Quick Reference Guide

MICROSOFT®
WORD 2000

REBECCA J. FIALA
JEFF GRISENTHWAITE
CATHY VESECKY

275 Madison Ave., NY, NY 10016
www.ddcpub.com

Managing Editor: Kathy Berkemeyer
Technical Editor: Don Mayo
Layout and Design: Julie Heskin

Copyright 1999 by DDC Publishing, Inc.

Published by DDC Publishing, Inc.

First DDC Publishing, Inc. Printing
10   9   8   7   6   5   4   3   2

Catalog No. G48

ISBN: 1-56243-634-1

Printed in the United States of America

TABLE OF CONTENTS

BASICS
Start Word 1
Exit Word 1
Window Controls 1
Shortcut Menus 4
Dialog Box Elements 5
Help 7

FILE MANAGEMENT
Word Documents 13
Open Document 15
Browse for Folders and Files 16
Close Document 19
Save Document 19
Print Document 22
Document Properties 23

NAVIGATE & SELECT
Document Navigation 25
Select Information 28

EDITING BASICS
Move Text 34
Copy Text 35
Office Clipboard 36
Delete Text 37
Overtype Mode 37
Undo/Redo 38

VIEW OPTIONS
Screen Views 40
Screen Elements 42

EDIT/FORMAT TEXT
AutoText 51
Backgrounds and Fills 53
Borders and Shading 59
Bullets and Numbering 64
Character Formatting 73
Editing Options 82
Fields 83
Headers/Footers 86
Macros 90
Newspaper–Style Columns 93
Page and Section Formatting 96

Table of Contents

Page Setup..98
Paragraph Formatting..105
Styles...110
Tabs...124

Word Objects
Graphic Objects..127
Text Boxes...144
WordArt...148

Tables
Table Basics...150
Table Text..164
Table Formula Basics..167
Table Formats..170

References
Bookmarks...171
Captions...172
Cross–References...174
Footnotes/Endnotes...175
Index and Tables..178

Proofing Tools
AutoCorrect..191
Comments..192
Find and Replace..195
Highlighter Pen...199
Hyphenation...200
Protect Document...202
Spelling and Grammar..203
Thesaurus..206
Track Changes...207
Word Count..211

Mail Options
Envelopes and Labels...212
Mail Merge...214

Word Online
Web Toolbar...227
Office Mail..229
Online Meeting...230
Discussions..232
Save Document as Web Page................................233

INTRODUCTION

What This Manual Covers

This manual is divided into 12 sections, moving alphabetically from basic to more advanced features.

Users who have been familiar with former versions of Microsoft Word will find many "old friends": background spell check, shortcut (right-click) menus, and quick file-switching via the taskbar, among others.

Several features in Word 2000 will be new to all users, however:

- **Streamlined display** of the Standard and Formatting toolbars which now share one row in the Word workspace.

- New, **personalized interface** wherein Word 2000 menus and toolbars display only those menu items and toolbar buttons you use most frequently.

- **Places bar** in the Open, Save, and Browse dialog boxes.

- **Collect and Paste**, which allows you to keep up to 12 items available on the clipboard.

- **Install on Demand**. This feature installs programs and components on an as-needed basis, saving hard drive space.

- **Migrating settings and roaming user profiles**, which allow you to keep the default and user-specific settings you have set in former versions of Word.

- **Coordinated themes and designs** throughout Office programs. For example, you will be able to match Word templates to presentations you create in PowerPoint.

- Online and Internet-based **collaboration** abilities.

- Integrated **e-mail capabilities**.

INTRODUCTION

BOOK CONVENTIONS

Command Examples

Procedures in this guide are composed of a series of numbered or lettered steps. You usually have a choice between using mouse or keyboard methods. In many instances, these methods are combined, as in the following example:

Click **File**..**Alt**+**F**

In cases where multiple mouse and/or keystroke methods are available for one task and cannot be provided together, the commands are broken down into separate subheadings (e.g., *Set Tab Using Ruler* and *Set Tab Using Menu*). Otherwise, they are divided by the word *OR*, as below:

1   Select text to copy.

2   Click **Copy** 🔲 on **Standard** toolbar ....**Ctrl**+**C**
     OR

     Click **Edit**, **Copy**..............................**Alt**+**E**,**C**

When you see a substitution word to the right of a step (e.g., *text, name, number*), type the required information or setting, such as a subject line, a file name, or a percentage.

In addition to the command procedures included in this Quick Reference Guide, other techniques for executing a given task often exist. The techniques listed here represent the fastest, most commonly used procedures.

START WORD

1 Click 🏁 **Start** .... 🔲

2 Point to 📁 **Programs** ▶ .... **P**

3 Click 📄 **Microsoft Word** .... ⬆⬇, **Enter**

EXIT WORD

Click **File**, **Exit** .... **Alt** + **F**, **X**

📖 *If you have not saved changes to the document, you will be prompted to do so.*

WINDOW CONTROLS

Maximize Window

Enlarges window to fill workspace.

Click **Maximize** 🔲 .... **Ctrl** + **F10**
in upper–right corner of window.

Minimize Window

Reduces window to a taskbar button.

Click **Minimize** 🗕 in upper–right corner of window.

Restore Window

Returns a maximized window to its former size. After restoring a window, the Maximize button appears.

Click **Restore** 🗗 .... **Ctrl** + **F5**
in upper–right corner of maximized window.

BASICS

Arrange All Windows

Arranges multiple document windows vertically on the screen.

Click **Window**, **Arrange All** ....

Next Window

Click desired Word document on taskbar ....

Move Window

 *A maximized window must be restored before it can be moved (see **Restore Window**, page 1).*

1 Position arrow pointer on title bar of active window.

2 Click and drag window to desired position.

Resize Window

 *A maximized window must be restored before it can be sized (see **Restore Window**, page 1).*

1 Position arrow pointer on border or corner of window.

The arrow pointer changes to a sizing arrow: ↔

2 Click and drag window to desired size.

New Window

Opens a new window containing contents of active document.

 Any editing or formatting performed in one window of a document is copied in all other windows of that document.

Click **Window**, **New Window** ....

Split Window

Splits a document window into two panes, allowing you to view and edit two different parts of the document simultaneously.

1   Click **Window**, **Split** ....

    The arrow pointer changes to a pane sizing arrow ⇕ and is positioned in the middle of the screen, on top of the split bar:

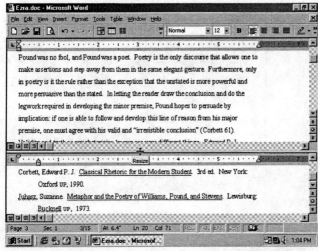

2   Drag mouse to move split bar ....

3   Click mouse button when split bar reaches desired position.

    To remove split:

    Double-click split bar .... **Alt**+**W**, **S**

SHORTCUT MENUS

Many Word 2000 features can be quickly accessed from shortcut menus which provide context-sensitive commands.

Shortcut menus are most commonly accessed by right–clicking the mouse button, but they may also be opened by pressing the **Applications** *key or by pressing* **Shift+F10**. *Shortcut menus are frequently used in conjunction with background spelling check:*

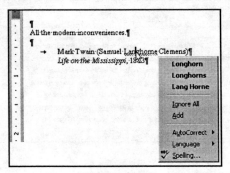

SHORTCUT MENU

DIALOG BOX ELEMENTS

When Word needs additional information to complete a menu command, a dialog box appears. An ellipsis (…) following a menu item indicates that a dialog box will open. Dialog boxes may contain the following elements:

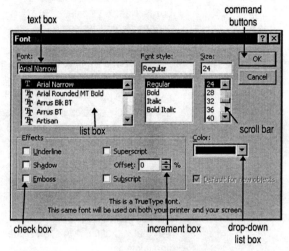

check box	Provides a space where you can select or deselect an option. A selected check box contains a check mark. More than one check box may be selected at a time in a group.
command buttons	Carry out actions described in the button's name, such as Apply, Save, or Open.
drop-down list box	Provides a *drop-down arrow* you can click to open and select an item from the list.
increment box	Provides a space for typing a value. *Increment arrows* give you a way to select a value with the mouse. Also known as *spin box*.

continued…

DIALOG BOX ELEMENTS (CONT.)

list box

Displays a list of items from which selections can be made. A list box may have a *scroll bar* that can be used to show hidden items in the list.

named tabs

Found at the top of some dialog boxes. Named tabs categorize options by the tab's name.

Preview box

Often found on the right-hand side of a dialog box. A Preview box provides a graphic representation of a selected item or style as it will look in your document once the change is applied. These boxes are not always named.

radio buttons

Circle-shaped buttons that mark options in a set. You can select only one option from the set. Also known as *option buttons*.

scroll bar

Provides *scroll arrows* and a *scroll box* that you can use to show hidden items in a list.

text box

Provides a space for typing in information.

When selecting commands in Word 2000 dialog boxes, you can often activate dialog box changes by double-clicking the desired setting. Doing so closes the dialog box and activates the change.

HELP

*There are two basic Microsoft Word Help modes in Word 2000—one of which makes use of the Office Assistant and the other which is the standard Microsoft Word Help window with an index format. If you keep the Office Assistant displayed, complete the procedure below. If your Office Assistant is hidden, see **Microsoft Word Help Window**, page 10.*

Office Assistant

The Office Assistant is an animated on–screen character that anticipates questions you may have according to the task you seem to be performing. You can customize the Office Assistant by selecting a character from the Gallery and setting options for how the Assistant will help you.

1 Click Office Assistant F1

   OR

   Click **Microsoft Word Help** on **Standard** toolbar.

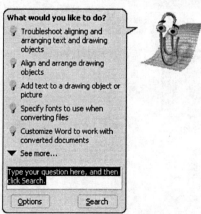

  Your Office Assistant may be a different character.

continued...

OFFICE ASSISTANT (CONT.)

 Your Office Assistant suggests some topics that may help you. If you wish to select one of these, skip to step 4.

2   Type a question, or a keyword or phrase, in text box.

3   Click  .... Enter

4   Click the help topic that best answers your question.

OR

Navigate through Help windows using the **Back** and **Forward** buttons.

To print topic:

a   Click

*The **Print** dialog box appears.*

b   Select desired print options. *(See **Print Document**, page 22.)*

c   Click OK .... Enter

To go to Microsoft Word Help Window:

Click Show

*(See **Microsoft Word Help Window**, page 10.)*

SHOW/HIDE OFFICE ASSISTANT

HIDE OFFICE ASSISTANT

Hides Office Assistant temporarily. If you press F1 at any time, the Office Assistant reappears.

Right-click Office Assistant, then .... `Alt` + `H`, `O`
click **Hide [Office Assistant]**.

TURN OFF OFFICE ASSISTANT

Hides the Office Assistant for the current user in all future sessions. If you press the F1 key, the Microsoft Word Help window appears—not the Office Assistant.

1 Right-click Office Assistant.

2 Click **Options** .... `O`

3 Deselect **Use the Office Assistant** check box ..... `U`

4 Click [OK] .... `Enter`

SPECIFY WHEN OFFICE ASSISTANT APPEARS

The Office Assistant pops up whenever you perform certain actions.

1 Right-click Office Assistant.

2 Click **Options** .... `O`

3 Select/deselect options as desired to specify when Office Assistant will appear automatically:

continued...

BASICS

SPECIFY WHEN OFFICE ASST. APPEARS (CONT.)

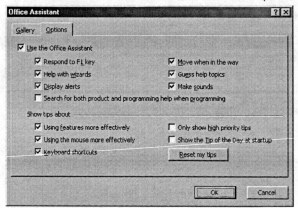

📖 *You can deselect all options if you do not want the Office Assistant to appear under any circumstance.*

4 Click OK .... Enter

Microsoft Word Help Window

Appears if you request help after turning off the Office Assistant, or if you click the Show button when navigating through Help windows.

1 Select desired help format from the following named tabs:

- **Contents** tab.. Alt + C

    Allows you to view Word 2000 Help topics in a table-of-contents format.

    a Click plus sign next to desired general topic.

    b Click Help page icon ? next to desired specific topic.

    *Selected Help topic appears in the right pane of the **Microsoft Word Help** window.*

- **A**nswer Wizard tab.............................. Alt + A

  Follow on-screen prompts.

- **I**ndex tab .... Alt + I

  > *Many people find the Index tab to be the*
  > *fastest way to get help in this window. If*
  > *you're uncertain of which tab to try, you*
  > *might like to start here.*

  Follow on-screen prompts.

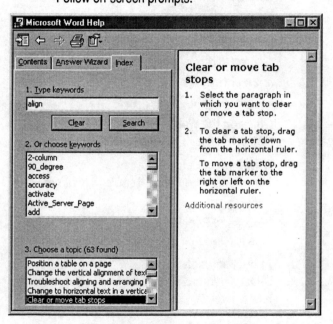

2 Navigate through Help windows using the **Back** and **Forward** buttons.

   To display more options:

   Click **Options**

3 Click **Close** ☒ to close **Microsoft Word Help** window.

BASICS

Get Help from the Help Menu

The Help menu allows you to access help information from a number of different sources.

1   Click **Help** .... **Alt**+**H**

2   Select desired help source:

-   **Microsoft Word Help**
    *(See **Office Assistant**, page 7, or **Microsoft Word Help Window**, page 10.)*

-   **Show/Hide the Office Assistant**

-   **What's This**
    *Changes the arrow pointer to a context-sensitive help arrow pointer: *↖?* . Simply click on screen elements to display ScreenTips.*

-   **Office on the Web**
    Connects you to Microsoft's home page.

-   **WordPerfect Help**
    Provides help performing WordPerfect tasks in Word 2000.

-   **Detect and Repair**
    Tries to detect and fix errors.

-   **About Microsoft Word**
    Displays software, system, and technical support information.

Dialog Box Help

1   Click question mark button 🔲 in upper-right corner of dialog box.

    *The arrow pointer changes to a context-sensitive help arrow pointer: *↖?**

2   Click screen element to view ScreenTip.

FILE MANAGEMENT

WORD DOCUMENTS

Create New Document

Click **New Blank Document** 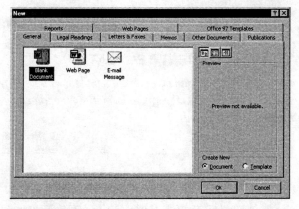 .... **Ctrl** + **N**
on **Standard** toolbar.

Templates

*A **template** stores settings and formatting which you can apply to an existing file or use to create a new file.*

NORMAL.DOT is the global template that contains information that is available to all Word documents.

Word provides preformatted templates for a number of different document types.

CREATE NEW DOCUMENT BASED ON TEMPLATE

1   Click **File**, **New** .... **Alt** + **F**, **N**

2   Click named tab containing template to use to create new document.

3   Click desired template.

4   Click **OK** .... **Enter**

FILE MANAGEMENT

CREATE NEW TEMPLATE

1   Click **File**, **New** .... `Alt`+`F`,`N`

2   Select **Template** radio button .... `Alt`+`T`

3   Click [OK] .... `Enter`

CREATE NEW TEMPLATE BASED ON DOCUMENT

1   Display document to base new template on.

2   Click **File**, **Save As** .... `Alt`+`F`,`A`

3   Type new template **File name** .... *filename*

4   Click **Save as type** drop-down arrow and select **Document Template (*.dot)**.

*The **Templates** folder appears in the **Save in** text box. All templates saved in this folder will appear in the General tab of the **New** dialog box (File, New).*

5   Click [Save] .... `Enter`

ATTACH DOCUMENT TEMPLATE

Replaces the active document's current template with another template of your choice. Document formatting is updated automatically, if desired.

1   Click **Tools** .... `Alt`+`T`

2   Click **Templates and Add–Ins** .... `I`

*The template currently attached to the active document is displayed in the **Document template** text box.*

3   Type name of **Document template** to attach.

OR

FILE MANAGEMENT

a Click 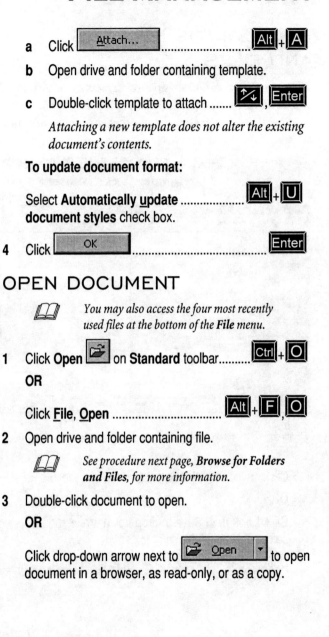 Attach... .... **Alt** + **A**

b Open drive and folder containing template.

c Double-click template to attach ...... **↑↓** , **Enter**

Attaching a new template does not alter the existing document's contents.

To update document format:

Select **Automatically update** .... **Alt** + **U**
document styles check box.

4 Click OK .... **Enter**

OPEN DOCUMENT

📖 *You may also access the four most recently used files at the bottom of the **File** menu.*

1 Click **Open** 📂 on **Standard** toolbar.......... **Ctrl** + **O**
OR

Click **File**, **Open** .... **Alt** + **F** , **O**

2 Open drive and folder containing file.

📖 *See procedure next page, **Browse for Folders and Files**, for more information.*

3 Double-click document to open.
OR

Click drop-down arrow next to 📂 **Open** ▾ to open document in a browser, as read-only, or as a copy.

FILE MANAGEMENT

BROWSE FOR FOLDERS AND FILES

When you open a document, save a document for the first time, or use other commands that require you to specify a file location, Word displays a dialog box that you can use to browse folders.

✍ FROM BROWSE, OPEN, OR SAVE DIALOG BOX

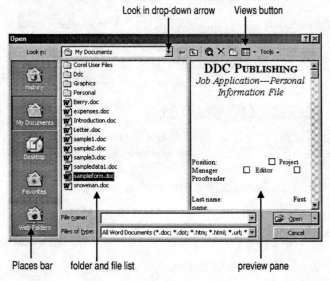

Look in drop-down arrow   Views button

Places bar   folder and file list   preview pane

1   Click an icon on **Places bar** to open desired folder.

OR

Click **Look in** or **Save in** drop-down arrow and select desired drive and/or folder.

2   Double–click folders in folder list to open them, as necessary.

FILE MANAGEMENT

Navigate Folders when Browsing

Back ⬅	`Alt`+`1`	Return to previous folder.
Up One Level 🔼	`Alt`+`2`	Go to parent folder of current folder.
Search the Web 🔍	`Alt`+`3`	Perform an online search.
Delete ✖	`Del`	Sends folder or file to Recycle Bin.
Create New Folder 📁	`Alt`+`5`	Add new folder to current folder.
Views ▦▾	*n/a*	Display files as **List**, **Details**, **Properties**, or **Preview**.

To add file or folder to Favorites:

a Select file or folder.

b Click **Tools**, **Add to Favorites**.... `Alt`+`L`,`A`

 *To search for a file or folder, see **Find Files When Browsing** on the following page.*

FILE MANAGEMENT

Find Files when Browsing

⌖ FROM BROWSE, OPEN, OR SAVE DIALOG BOX

1 Click **Tools**, **Find** .... **Alt** + **L** , **F**

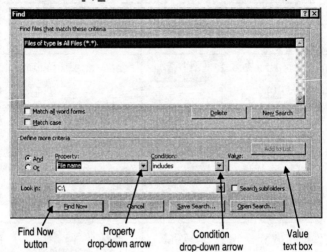

Find Now button — Property drop-down arrow — Condition drop-down arrow — Value text box

2 Click **Property** drop-down arrow and select **File name** or **Files of type**.

If searching for a filename:

Click **Value** text box and type desired filename.

If searching for a file type:

Click **Condition** drop-down arrow and select file type.

3 Click **Add to List** .... **Alt** + **A**

4 Repeat steps 2 and 3 to add more search criteria, if necessary.

5 Click **Look in** drop-down arrow and select drive and/or folder to search.

6 Select **Search subfolders** check box .... **Alt** + **H** to search subfolders of drive or folder.

7 Click **Find Now** .... **Alt** + **F**

18

FILE MANAGEMENT

CLOSE DOCUMENT

Click **File**, **Close** .... `Ctrl`+`W`

If you have not saved changes to the document, you will be prompted to do so.

Close All Documents

1 Hold **Shift** and click **File** menu.

2 Click **Close All** .... `C`

   OR

   Click **Save All** .... `L`

*Click the **Yes** or **No** button to save and close each file, if they already have filenames. If a file has not been named, the **Save As** dialog box appears. (See **Save Document**, below.)*

SAVE DOCUMENT

*See also **Save Document as Web Page** in the Word Online section, page 233.*

*To password-protect your document, click **General Options** in the **Tools** menu available in the **Save As** dialog box. From the Save tab, several **File sharing options** are available to you, including: passwords to open and/or modify, and read only. (See also **Protect Document**, page 202.)*

1 Click **Save** 🖫 on **Standard** toolbar .... `Ctrl`+`S`

   OR

   Click **File**, **Save** .... `Alt`+`F`,`S`

If you have saved this file previously, you can stop here; changes to the file have been saved. If this is the first time you have saved this file, proceed to step 2.

continued…

FILE MANAGEMENT

SAVE DOCUMENT (CONT.)

2 Type document **File name** in text box.

3 Open drive and folder to save in.

> *See **Browse for Folders and Files**, page 16, for more information.*

To change file type:

a Click **Save as type** drop-down arrow `Alt`+`T`

b Select format to save as.................... `↑↓`, `Enter`

4 Click `💾 Save` .... `Alt`+`S`

Save Copy of Document (Save As)

1 Click **File**, **Save As** .... `Alt`+`F`, `A`

2 Follow steps 2-4, **Save Document**, above, changing the filename, file type, and/or storage location.

VERSIONS

Allows you to save multiple versions of one document in one file.

SAVE VERSION

1 Click **Save Version** 🖳 .... `Alt`+`F`, `E`
on **Reviewing** toolbar.

> *If you use the toolbar method, skip to step 3.*

To create new version on each save:

Select **Automatically save a version on close** check box.

2 Click `Save Now...` .... `Enter`

3 Type **Comments on version**, as desired.

The date, time, and the current user's name appear by default.

4 Click `OK`

FILE MANAGEMENT

WORK WITH VERSIONS

1 Click **File**, V**e**rsions .... `Alt`+`F`, `E`

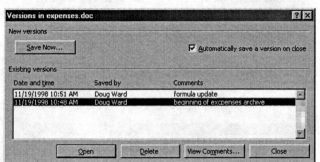

2 Select version to work with .... `Alt`+`T`, `↑↓`
from **Existing versions**.

3 Select desired command button action(s).

FILE MANAGEMENT

PRINT DOCUMENT

*The **Print** dialog box does not appear when you use the **Print** button on the toolbar.*

To print document using current settings:

Click **Print** 🖨 on **Standard** toolbar.

1   Click **File**, **Print** .... Ctrl + P

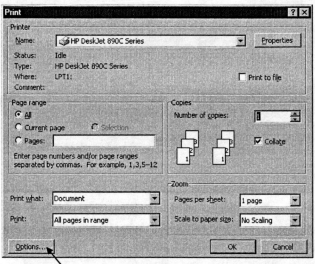

Click to see more print options.

2   Select desired **Print range** option, if necessary:

- **All** .... Alt + A

- **Current page** .... Alt + E

- **Selection** .... Alt + S

- **Pages** .... Alt + G, *page numbers*

FILE MANAGEMENT

📖 *To print a selection, you must highlight a portion of your document before opening the **Print** dialog box.*

3 Type **Number of copies** to print, if necessary.

4 Click [OK] .... Enter
to close **Print** dialog box and begin printing.

Printer Setup

1 Click **File**, **Print** .... Ctrl + P

2 Click **Name** drop-down arrow and select desired printer.

3 Click [Properties] .... Alt + P

4 Select desired options under each named tab.

📖 *The options available depend on the printer you selected.*

5 Click [OK] twice .... Enter, Enter

DOCUMENT PROPERTIES

Document properties are details about a file that help differentiate it from other files.

Display Document Properties

1 Click **File**, **Properties** .... Alt + F, I

2 Select desired properties tab.

3 Click [OK] .... Enter

FILE MANAGEMENT

Store Summary Information

1 Click **File**, **Properties**.......................... Alt + F , I

2 Click **Summary** tab, if necessary .... Ctrl + Tab

3 Enter summary information as desired:

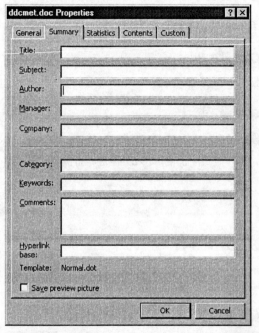

4 Click OK .... Enter

NAVIGATE & SELECT

DOCUMENT NAVIGATION

Go To Command

1 Double-click on left half of status bar............ **Ctrl**+**G**

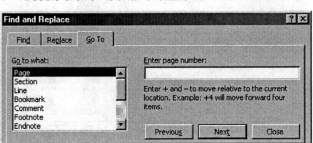

*The default **Go to what** item is* Page.

2 Type number of page to go to............................ *number*
in **Enter page number** text box.

To go to another document item:

   a Select type of document item ..... **Alt**+**O**, **⬍**
     to go to in **Go to what** list box.

   b Click **Enter [item number/name]** .... **Alt**+**E**
     text box.

   c Type number of name .... *number* or *name*
     of item to go to.

3 Click **Go To** .... **Alt**+**T**

   OR

Navigate through instances of document item:

  ■ **Previous** .... **Alt**+**S** or **Enter**

  ■ **Next** .... **Alt**+**T** or **Enter**

4 Click **Close** .... **Esc**

NAVIGATE & SELECT

Navigation Shortcuts

MOVE	SHORTCUT
Left one character	←
Right one character	→
Left one word	Ctrl + ←
Right one word	Ctrl + →
Up one paragraph	Ctrl + ↑
Down one paragraph	Ctrl + ↓
Left one newspaper–style column	Alt + ↑
Right one newspaper–style column	Alt + ↓
Up one line	↑
Down one line	↓
Beginning of line	Home
End of line	End
Up one screen	Page Up
Down one screen	Page Down
Top of previous page	Ctrl + Page Up
Bottom of next page	Ctrl + Page Down
Beginning of document	Ctrl + Home
End of document	Ctrl + End
Last revision	Shift + F5

NAVIGATE & SELECT

Table Navigation Shortcuts

MOVE   **SHORTCUT**

Next cell .... `Tab`

*If cursor is in last cell, pressing the **Tab** key adds another row.*

Previous cell... `Shift` + `Tab`

Up one row.. `↑`

Down one row... `↓`

Left one character .... `←`

Right one character... `→`

First cell current row................................... `Alt` + `Home`

Last cell current row..................................... `Alt` + `End`

First cell current column.......................... `Alt` + `Page Up`

Last cell current column......................... `Alt` + `Page Down`

NAVIGATE & SELECT

SELECT INFORMATION

Select Document Text

SELECT ENTIRE DOCUMENT

Click **Edit, Select All**..

SELECT TEXT USING MOUSE

SELECT	ACTION
Any item	Drag over text.
Word	Double–click word.
Line of text	Position arrow pointer left of line and click.
Multiple lines of text	Position arrow pointer left of first line and drag to last line.
Sentence	Hold **Ctrl** and click anywhere in sentence.
Paragraph	Double–click to left of paragraph.
Entire document	Position pointer left of text and triple–click.
Vertical block of text	Hold **Alt** and drag over text.

   *You can also select information by placing cursor at starting point, holding down **Shift**, and clicking at end of desired selection.*

NAVIGATE & SELECT

Select Text Using Keyboard

SELECT	SHORTCUT
Up one line	Shift + ↑
Down one line	Shift + ↓
Left one character	Shift + ←
Right one character	Shift + →
Beginning of word	Shift + Ctrl + ←
End of word	Shift + Ctrl + →
Beginning of line	Shift + Home
End of line	Shift + End
Beginning of paragraph	Shift + Ctrl + ↑
End of paragraph	Shift + Ctrl + ↓
Up one screen	Shift + Page Up
Down one screen	Shift + Page Down
Beginning of document	Shift + Ctrl + Home
End of document	Shift + Ctrl + End
Entire document	Ctrl + A

NAVIGATE & SELECT

Select Graphic Object

1   Click **Select Objects** on **Drawing** toolbar.

2   Position arrow pointer on object to select.

The arrow pointer changes to a move pointer:

3   Click mouse button.

The selected object is surrounded by eight sizing handles:

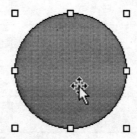

To deselect object(s):

Click blank area in workspace............................

SELECT MULTIPLE OBJECTS

1   Click **Select Objects** on **Drawing** toolbar.

2   Click first object to select.

3   Press and hold down **Shift**........................ **Shift** + *click*
    while selecting subsequent objects.

OR

1   Click **Select Objects** on **Drawing** toolbar.

2   Click and drag arrow pointer from one corner of objects
    to opposite corner.

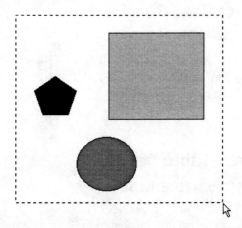

3 Release mouse button when all objects are within dashed rectangle.

Each object within dashed rectangle is selected.

To deselect object from those selected:

Press and hold down **Shift** .... `Shift` +*click*
and click object to deselect.

Select Text Box

Click text box border.

*When a text box is selected, the **Text Box** toolbar appears, the arrow pointer changes to a move pointer, and the text box border appears, as do eight object handles:*

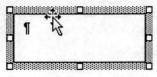

NAVIGATE & SELECT

Select Text Box Object

Click object inside text box.

When text box object is selected, the text box border appears, as do eight object handles:

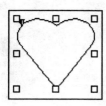

Select Table Data

SELECT ENTIRE TABLE

💣 *The Num Lock key must be turned off.*

1 Place cursor in table to select.

2 Press **Alt+5** *(NumPad)* .... **Alt** + **5**

   OR

   a Click **Table**, **Select** .... **Alt** + **A**, **C**

   b Click **Table** .... **T**

SELECT COLUMN

Hold down the **Alt** key and click .... **Alt** + *click*
mouse button in cell of column to select.

OR

1 Position arrow pointer above column until it changes to a solid, down-pointing arrow: ⬇

2 Click mouse button.

OR

1 Place cursor in column to select.

2 Click **Table**, **Select** .... **Alt** + **A**, **C**

3 Click **Column** .... **C**

NAVIGATE & SELECT

SELECT ROW

Click mouse button in selection bar to left of row to select.

The arrow pointer points to the right when it is placed in the selection bar: ⭿

SELECT CELL

Triple-click inside cell to select .... `Alt` + `A`,`C`,`E`

EDITING BASICS

MOVE TEXT

Cut and Paste

1 Select text to cut.

2 Click **Cut** ✂ on **Standard** toolbar .... `Ctrl`+`X`

  OR

  Click **Edit**, **Cut** .... `Alt`+`E`, `T`

  To paste in another Office document:

  Open document in which to paste text in its
  source application.

3 Place cursor where you wish to paste cut text.

4 Click **Paste** 📋 on **Standard** toolbar .... `Ctrl`+`V`

  OR

  Click **Edit**, **Paste** .... `Alt`+`E`, `P`

Drag and Drop (Move Text)

📖 *Drag-and-drop text editing can be
    enabled/disabled in the Edit tab of the
    Options dialog box (Tools, Options).*

1 Select text to move.

2 Click and hold down mouse button, dragging the drag-
    and-drop pointer 🔲 to new text location.

3 Position drag-and drop pointer where you want to
    insert text.

4 Release mouse button.

COPY TEXT

Copy and Paste

1   Select text to copy.

2   Click **Copy** 📋 on **Standard** toolbar.......... `Ctrl`+`C`

    OR

    Click **Edit**, **Copy** .... `Alt`+`E`, `C`

3   Place cursor where you wish to paste copied text.

4   Click **Paste** 📋 on **Standard** toolbar .... `Ctrl`+`V`

    OR

    Click **Edit**, **Paste** .... `Alt`+`E`, `P`

Drag and Drop (Copy Text)

📖   *Drag-and-drop text editing can be*
        enabled/disabled in the Edit tab of the
        Options *dialog box (Tools, Options).*

1   Select text to copy.

2   Press and hold down **Ctrl** .... `Ctrl`+*drag*
    while you click and drag the drag-and-drop

    pointer to new text location.

3   Position drag-and-drop pointer where you want to place
    copied text.

4   Release mouse button and the **Ctrl** key.

EDITING BASICS

OFFICE CLIPBOARD

*The **Office Clipboard** toolbar allows you to place up to 12
items on the Clipboard and paste any number of them into any
Office document. When you place two or more items on the
Clipboard, the Clipboard toolbar automatically appears.*

*To place an item on the Clipboard, follow standard cut or copy
procedures (see **Move Text**, page 34; or **Copy Text**, page 35). To
display Clipboard toolbar, see **Display/Hide Toolbar**, page 42.*

1   Position arrow pointer over Clipboard item to paste.

A ScreenTip displays the item's contents or file type:

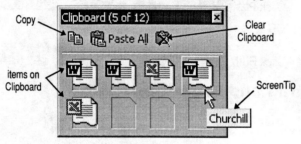

2   Click Clipboard item to paste.

> *You may need to format items copied in other
> Office programs after you paste them into a
> Word 2000 document.*

Paste All Items from Office Clipboard

Click on **Clipboard** toolbar .... **Alt**+**L**

Clear Office Clipboard

Click **Clear Clipboard** 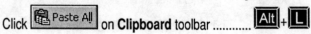 on **Clipboard** toolbar.

EDITING BASICS

DELETE TEXT

1 Select text to delete.

2 Click **Edit**, **Clear** .... `Delete` or `Backspace`

OVERTYPE MODE

*The **OVR** indicator on the status bar is bold when Overtype mode is active.*

> *Overtype mode can be enabled/disabled in the Edit tab of the **Options** dialog box (Tools, Options).*

Double–click **OVR** indicator `OVR` or `OVR` .... `Insert` on status bar.

> *You can also type directly over existing text by selecting it and typing.*

Editing Basics

Undo/Redo

Undo Most Recent Command

Click **Undo [command]** .... **Ctrl** + **Z**
on **Standard** toolbar.

OR

Click **Edit**, **Undo** .... **Alt** + **E**, **U**

Undo Series of Commands

1 Click **Undo [command]** drop-down arrow

2 Select sequence of commands to undo.

> *Commands will be highlighted as you move the
> mouse downward. All commands that are
> highlighted when you click the mouse button
> will be undone.*

Redo Last Undo Command

*To reverse an Undo command, you must not perform any
actions after undoing it.*

Click **Redo [command]** **F4**
on **Standard** toolbar.

OR

Click **Edit**, **Redo** .... **Ctrl** + **Y**

Redo Series of Commands

1   Click **Redo [command]** drop-down arrow

2   Select sequence of commands to redo.

> *Commands will be highlighted as you move the mouse downward. All commands that are highlighted when you click the mouse button will be redone.*

VIEW OPTIONS

SCREEN VIEWS

Normal View

Click **Normal View** ▤ .... `Alt` + `V`, `N`
on status bar.

Web Layout View

Click **Web Layout View** ▣ .... `Alt` + `V`, `W`
on status bar.

Print Layout View

Click **Print Layout View** ▣ .... `Alt` + `V`, `P`
on status bar.

Outline View

Click **Outline View** ▤ .... `Alt` + `V`, `O`
on status bar.

Full Screen View

Click **V**iew, F**u**ll Screen .... `Alt` + `V`, `U`

> **To exit Full Screen view:**

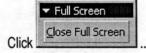

Click .... `Esc`

Print Preview

Click **Print Preview** ▤ .... `Alt` + `F`, `V`
on **Standard** toolbar.

> **To exit Print Preview:**

Click **Close Preview** .... `Alt` + `C`

Zoom

SET ZOOM USING MOUSE

1   Click drop–down arrow next to **Zoom** `100%` on **Standard** toolbar.

2   Select or type desired magnification percentage.

SET ZOOM USING MENU

1   Click **View**, **Zoom** .... **Alt** + **V**, **Z**

2   Select desired **Zoom to** option.

   OR

   a   Select **Many pages** radio button .... **M**

   b   Click **Multiple Pages**  .... **Tab**

   c   Drag across page layout palette to desired number of pages to view, then click.

   To adjust custom magnification setting:

   Click **Percent** increment box and enter/select desired magnification percentage.

3   Click 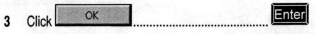 **OK** .... **Enter**

VIEW OPTIONS

SCREEN ELEMENTS

Toolbars

*In Word 2000, the **Standard** and **Formatting** toolbars are combined on one row and are personalized like menus. The first time Word is launched, the toolbar displays only the most basic options. As you continue working in Word, the buttons that you do not use are replaced with those you do.*

*For some procedures in this book, you will need to access hidden buttons with the **More Buttons** arrow (see **Access a Hidden Button**, below). See also **Menus**, page 47, for more information on personalized options in Word 2000. See also **Organizer**, page 117.*

DISPLAY/HIDE TOOLBAR

In addition to any custom toolbars you may have created, Word 2000 provides 16 toolbars that contain buttons commonly used to perform specific tasks.

1   Right-click any toolbar .... `Alt`+`V`, `T`

2   Select/deselect toolbar to display/hide.

MORE TOOLBAR BUTTONS

ACCESS A HIDDEN BUTTON

*Allows you to use buttons that are not visible on a toolbar. Hidden buttons would appear if the toolbar were resized. (See also **Size Toolbar**, page 45.)*

1   Click **More Buttons** arrow
    on toolbar containing button.

2   Click desired button.

VIEW OPTIONS

ADD/REMOVE TOOLBAR BUTTON

1   Click **More Buttons** arrow 🔢 on toolbar with button to
    add or remove.

2   Click **Add or Remove Buttons**.............................. $\boxed{A}$

3   Click button to add or remove.

    If button is not displayed:

    a   Click **Customize** .... $\boxed{C}$, $\boxed{Enter}$

    b   Click **Commands** tab .... $\boxed{Alt}$+$\boxed{C}$
        if necessary.

    c   Select desired category .... $\boxed{Alt}$+$\boxed{G}$, $\boxed{⤢↓}$

    d   Drag button from **Commands** list box to desired
        position on toolbar.

        OR

        Drag button off toolbar to remove button.

    e   Click $\boxed{\text{Close}}$ .... $\boxed{Enter}$

VIEW OPTIONS

DISPLAY TOOLBARS ON SEPARATE LINES

1   Click **Tools, Customize**...................... `Alt`+`T`,`C`

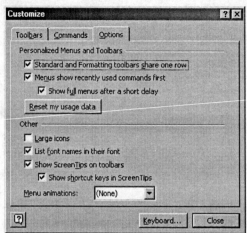

2   Click **Options** tab, if necessary................... `Alt`+`O`

3   Deselect **Standard and Formatting**........... `Alt`+`S`
    toolbars share one row check box.

4   Click | Close | .... `Enter`

MOVE/SIZE TOOLBAR

MOVE TOOLBAR

*You can move a toolbar onto the workspace to create a floating toolbar. Also, when the **Standard** and **Formatting** toolbars share one row, you may display more buttons on either toolbar by moving the **Formatting** toolbar handle to the left or right.*

1   Point to toolbar sizing handle

    The arrow pointer changes to a move pointer: ✛

2   Drag toolbar to desired location.

    As you drag the toolbar, its shape changes according to the area it occupies.

44

SIZE TOOLBAR

*You may resize floating toolbars only. If you wish to display more or fewer buttons on a docked toolbar, see **Move Toolbar**, previous page.*

1   Position arrow pointer on toolbar border.

    The arrow pointer changes to a sizing arrow: ↔

2   Click and drag toolbar to desired size.

CUSTOM TOOLBAR

CREATE CUSTOM TOOLBAR

1   Click **Tools**, **Customize** .... `Alt`+`T`, `C`

2   Click **Toolbars** tab, if necessary .... `Alt`+`B`

3   Click **New...** .... `Alt`+`N`

4   Type new **Toolbar name** in text box .... *toolbar*

5   Click **OK** .... `Enter`

    The new toolbar is a very small square since it does not yet contain buttons:

6   Click **Commands** tab .... `Alt`+`C`

7   Select desired category .... `Tab`, `↑/↓`

8   Drag buttons from the **Commands** list box onto the new toolbar.

9   Repeat steps 7 and 8 until all buttons are added as desired.

10 Click **Close** .... `Enter`

VIEW OPTIONS

DELETE CUSTOM TOOLBAR

1 Click **Tools**, **Customize** .... `Alt`+`T`,`C`

2 Click **Toolbars** tab, if necessary .... `Alt`+`B`

3 Highlight toolbar to delete .... `Tab` `↑↓`

4 Click **Delete** .... `Alt`+`D`

5 Click **OK** .... `Enter`

6 Click **Close**

TOOLBAR OPTIONS

1 Click **Tools**, **Customize** .... `Alt`+`T`,`C`

2 Click **Options** tab, if necessary .... `Alt`+`O`

3 Select/deselect desired toolbar options:

- **Large icons** .... `Alt`+`L`
  to increase toolbar button size.

- **List font names in their fonts** .... `Alt`+`F`

- **Show ScreenTips on toolbars** .... `Alt`+`T`

  📖 *ScreenTips display the names of buttons*
  when the arrow pointer is positioned over
  a toolbar button:

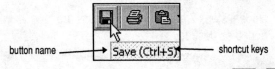

button name ──→ Save (Ctrl+S) ←── shortcut keys

- **Show shortcut keys in ScreenTips** .... `Alt`+`H`

4 Click **Close** .... `Enter`

Menus

*The personalized menus in Word 2000 put the features you use most frequently within easy reach. The first time Word is launched, the personalized menus display only the most basic options. More advanced menu options are hidden but can be accessed at any time. As you continue to work with Word 2000, the basic options that you do not use regularly are replaced with those you use most often. (See also **Toolbars**, page 42.)*

DISPLAY FULL MENU

Double-click menu to open.

The full menu is displayed. Advanced menu options are displayed against a lighter background.

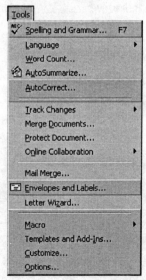

continued...

DISPLAY FULL MENU (CONT.)

OR

1 Click menu to open.

2 Point to expand arrows [⬇]

OR

Leave menu open for three seconds.

DISPLAY ALL FULL MENUS

Return to the menu format used in previous versions of Word.

1 Click **T**ools, **C**ustomize .... Alt + T , C

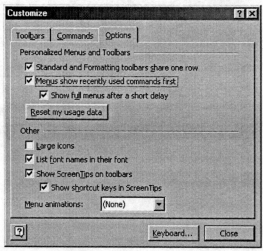

VIEW OPTIONS

2 Click **Options** tab, if necessary .... `Alt`+`O`

3 Deselect **Menus show recently used** .... `Alt`+`N`
commands first check box.

4 Click [Close] .... `Enter`

Rulers

Vertical rulers appear only in Print Layout view and Print Preview.

Click **View**, **Ruler** .... `Alt`+`V`, `R`

Nonprinting Characters

*(See **Screen Display Options**, on the following page, for information on displaying specific types of nonprinting characters.)*

Click **Show/Hide** ¶ [¶] .... `Shift`+`Ctrl`+`8`
on **Standard** toolbar.

VIEW OPTIONS

Screen Display Options

1. Click **Tools**, **Options** .... `Alt`+`T`,`O`

2. Click **View** tab, if necessary .... `Ctrl`+`Tab`

3. Select/deselect display options, as desired:

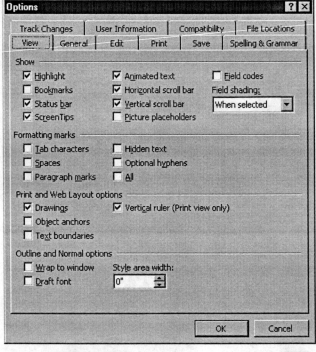

4. Click **OK** .... `Enter`

EDIT/FORMAT TEXT

AUTOTEXT

*(See also **Organizer**, page 117.)*

Create AutoText Entry

1 Select item to store as AutoText.

 *To store paragraph formatting in the AutoText entry, include the paragraph mark with the selected text. See **Nonprinting Characters**, page 49.*

2 Click **Insert**, **AutoText**, **New** ....

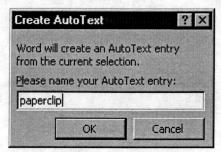

3 Name the new AutoText entry ....*name*

4 Click [OK] .... Enter

Insert AutoText Entry

INSERT AUTOTEXT ENTRY USING KEYBOARD

1 Place cursor in document where you want to insert an AutoText entry.

2 Type AutoText entry name ....*name*

3 Press **F3** F3

EDIT/FORMAT TEXT

INSERT AUTOTEXT ENTRY USING MENU

1 Place cursor where you want to insert AutoText entry.

2 Click **AutoText** 🖫 .... Alt + I , A , X
     on **AutoText** toolbar.

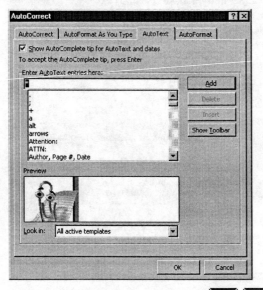

3 Double-click AutoText entry to insert....... ⬆⬇ , Enter

Delete AutoText Entry

1 Click **AutoText** 🖫 .... Alt + I , A , X
     on **AutoText** toolbar.

2 Select AutoText entry to delete .... ⬆⬇

3 Click Delete .... Alt + D

4 Click OK .... Enter

EDIT/FORMAT TEXT

BACKGROUNDS AND FILLS

Backgrounds

Backgrounds display only in Web Layout view.

1   Click **Format**, **Background**.................. `Alt`+`O`,`K`

2   Click desired background color on fill color palette.

> 📖 *See **Fill Effects**, page 54, and **More Fill Colors**, page 57.*

The document is moved into Web Layout view if you are in another view, and the selected background color appears.

THEMES

1   Click **Format**, **Theme**........................... `Alt`+`O`,`H`

2   Select desired theme from list box .... `↑/↓`

3   Click [OK   ] .... `Enter`

EDIT/FORMAT TEXT

Fill Effects

FILL WITH GRADIENT

1   Select object to fill with gradient.

2   Click **Fill Color** drop-down arrow 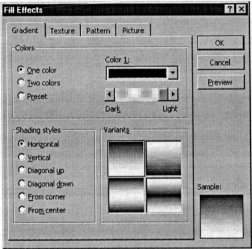 on **Drawing** toolbar.

3   Click **Fill Effects** .... **F**

4   Click **Gradient** tab, if necessary................................

5   **a**   Select **One color** radio button .... **Alt**+**O**

    b   Click **Color 1** drop-down arrow and select color.

    c   Drag **Dark/Light** scroll box .... **Alt**+**K**,

    OR

    a   Select **Two colors** radio button .... **Alt**+**T**

    b   Click **Color 1** drop-down arrow and select color.

    c   Click **Color 2** drop-down arrow and select color.

OR

a Select **Preset** radio button.................... <kbd>Alt</kbd>+<kbd>R</kbd>

b Click **Preset colors** drop-down arrow
and select desired color scheme.

6 Select from available **Shading styles**, if desired.

7 Select from available **Variants** .... <kbd>Alt</kbd>+<kbd>S</kbd>, <kbd>↔</kbd>
if desired.

8 Click <kbd>OK</kbd> .... <kbd>Enter</kbd>

FILL WITH TEXTURE

1 Select object to fill with texture.

2 Click **Fill Color** drop-down arrow 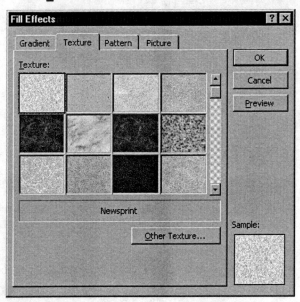 on **Drawing**
toolbar.

3 Click **Fill Effects**.. <kbd>F</kbd>

continued…

EDIT/FORMAT TEXT

FILL WITH TEXTURE (CONT.)

4   Click **Texture** tab, if necessary ....

5   Select desired **Texture**.................................... Tab,

6   Click OK .... Enter

FILL WITH PATTERN

1   Select object to fill with pattern.

2   Click **Fill Color** drop-down arrow on **Drawing** toolbar.

3   Click **Fill Effects** .... F

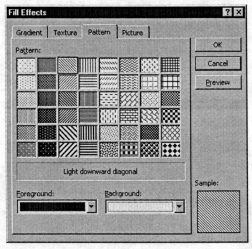

4   Click **Pattern** tab, if necessary ....

5   Select desired **Pattern** .... Tab,

   To edit pattern colors:

   a   Click **Foreground** drop-down arrow and select color.

   b   Click **Background** drop-down arrow and select color.

6   Click OK .... Enter

EDIT/FORMAT TEXT

FILL WITH PICTURE

1   Select object to fill with picture.

2   Click **Fill Color** drop-down arrow 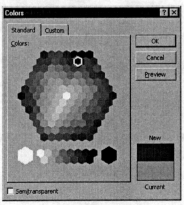 on **Drawing** toolbar.

3   Click <u>F</u>ill Effects... **F**

4   Click **Picture** tab, if necessary ....

5   Click [Se<u>l</u>ect Picture...] .... **Alt**+**L**

6   Open drive and folder containing picture file.

7   Double-click desired picture.

8   Click [OK] .... **Enter**

MORE FILL COLORS

STANDARD COLOR PALETTE

1   Select object to fill with color.

2   Click **Fill Color** drop-down arrow on **Drawing** toolbar.

3   Click <u>M</u>ore Fill Colors... **M**

continued…

STANDARD COLOR PALETTE (CONT.)

4   Click **Standard** tab, if necessary .... 🔀

5   Click desired color .... `Tab`, ↕

6   Click [OK] .... `Enter`

CUSTOM COLOR PALETTE

1   Select object to fill with color.

2   Click **Fill Color** drop-down arrow 🪣▾ on **Drawing** toolbar.

3   Click **More Fill Colors** .... Ⓜ

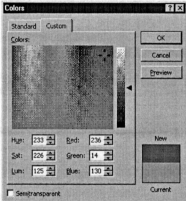

4   Click **Custom** tab, if necessary .... 🔀

5   Click desired color .... `Tab`, ↕
    OR
    Enter/select values in increment boxes as desired.

6   Drag triangle ◄ up or down **Colors** spectrum palette to
    lighten or darken selected color.
    To make fill color translucent:

    Select **Semitransparent** check box .... `Alt`+`I`

7   Click [OK] .... `Enter`

EDIT/FORMAT TEXT

BORDERS AND SHADING

Add Border

ADD BORDER USING TOOLBAR

1   Display **Tables and Borders** toolbar. (*See **Toolbars**, page 42.*)

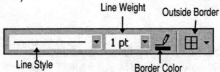

Line Weight   Outside Border

Line Style   Border Color

📖   *The name of the **Outside Border** button changes, depending on the last border style selected.*

2   Select item to frame.

3   Click **Line Style** drop-down arrow [⬛] and select desired border style.

   OR

   Click **Line Weight** drop-down arrow [½ ⬛] and select desired border width.

   OR

   Click **Border Color** [🖌] and select desired color or click **More Line Colors**.

4   Click **Outline Border** drop-down arrow [⊞⬛] and select border(s) to change:

   To delete border:

   Click **No Border**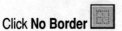

EDIT/FORMAT TEXT

ADD BORDER USING MENU

1   Select item to frame.

2   Click **Format**, **Borders and Shading**...... `Alt` + `O`, `B`

3   Click **Borders** tab, if necessary............................. `B`
    OR

    Click **Page Border** tab .... `P`
    to add borders around each page of document.

4   Select desired border style:

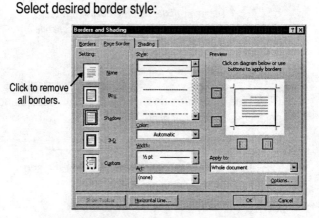

Click to remove all borders.

To add border to individual side(s) only:

a   Click 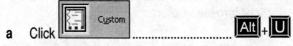 .... `Alt` + `U`

b   Click border elements directly on **Preview** diagram,
    or use Border dialog box buttons, to apply borders
    as desired:

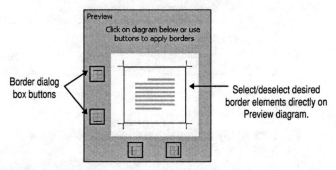

Border dialog box buttons

Select/deselect desired border elements directly on Preview diagram.

*Borders display in selected location(s) on **Preview** diagram.*

5 Click border **Style** list box .... `Tab`, `↑↓`
   and select desired border style.

6 Click **Color** drop-down arrow .... `↑↓`, `Enter`
   and select desired border color.

   To specify position of border on page:

   a Click Options... .... `Alt` + `O`

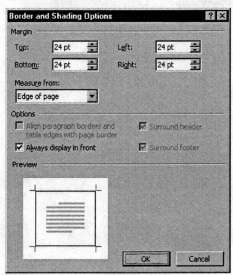

continued...

EDIT/FORMAT TEXT

  b Select desired location options.

  c Click [OK] .... [Enter]

7 Click **<u>W</u>idth** drop-down arrow and select desired border (points) width.

8 Click **Apply to** drop-down arrow and select desired border placement.

9 Click [OK] .... [Enter]

Add Shading/Color

ADD SHADING/COLOR USING TOOLBAR

1 Select item to apply shading to.

2 Click drop-down arrow next to **Shading Color** [icon] on **Tables and Borders** toolbar.

3 Click desired shading color on drop-down palette.

  To apply same color to another item:

  a Select next item to apply shading to.

  b Click **Shading Color** [icon]

EDIT/FORMAT TEXT

ADD SHADING/COLOR USING MENU

1 Select item to add shading to.

2 Click **Format**, **Borders and Shading** ......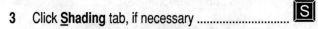

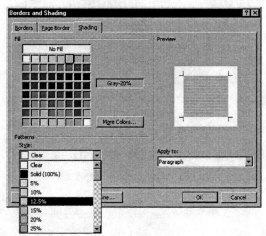

3 Click **Shading** tab, if necessary .... [S]

4 Select desired **Fill** and **Patterns** settings.

To apply shading/color to multiple objects:

a Click [Show Toolbar] ....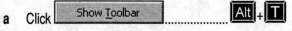

b See procedure above.

5 Click **Apply to** drop-down arrow and select desired shading placement.

6 Click [OK] ....  Enter

Edit/Format Text

BULLETS AND NUMBERING

Insert Bullets or Numbering

INSERT BULLETS OR NUMBERING USING TOOLBAR

1   Select text to format as bulleted or numbered list.

2   Click **Bullets** on **Formatting** toolbar.

   OR

   Click **Numbering** on **Formatting** toolbar.

INSERT BULLETS USING MENU

1   Select text to format as bulleted list.

2   Click **Format** .... **Alt**+**O**

3   Click **Bullets and Numbering** .... **N**

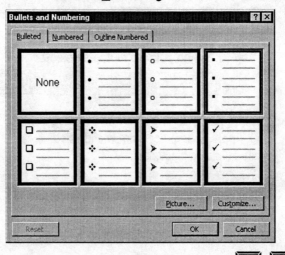

4   Click **Bulleted** tab, if necessary .... **Alt**+**B**

5   Click desired bullet format from palette.

6   Click **OK** .... **Enter**

EDIT/FORMAT TEXT

INSERT NUMBERING USING MENU

1. Select text to format as numbered/lettered list.

2. Click **Format**.. `Alt`+`O`

3. Click **Bullets and Numbering** .... `N`

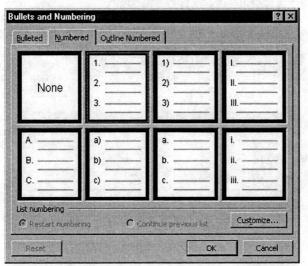

4. Click **Numbered** tab, if necessary .... `Alt`+`N`

5. Click desired number/letter format from palette.

   OR

   Click **None** to remove numbers/letters from selected text.

6. Click [OK] .... `Enter`

EDIT/FORMAT TEXT

Customize Bullets or Numbering

CUSTOMIZE BULLETED LIST

1 Click **F**or**mat** .... **Alt**+**O**

2 Click **Bullets and Numbering** .... **N**

3 Click **Bulleted** tab, if necessary .... **Alt**+**B**

4 Click bullet format to customize, if necessary.

5 Click **Customize...** .... **Alt**+**T**

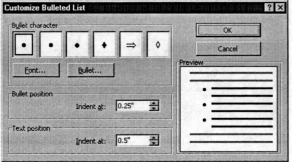

6 Select desired **Bullet character** ....

EDIT/FORMAT TEXT

To change font for selected bullet format:

a Click [Font...] .... Alt + F

b Select desired font, style, and point size.

c Click [OK] .... Enter

To select bullet character not in current palette:

a Click [Bullet...] .... Alt + B

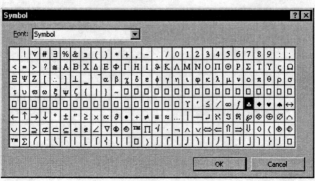

continued...

CUSTOMIZE BULLETED LIST (CONT.)

b Click **Font** drop-down arrow and select font set containing character to use as a bullet.

> *Click once on a bullet character to magnify it for easier viewing.*

c Double–click desired bullet character.

To modify *Bullet position*:

Click **Indent at** increment box .... `Alt`+`A`, `↕`
and enter/select desired bullet position.

> *To remove bullet indent altogether, type 0 (zero).*

To modify *Text position*:

Click **Indent at** increment box .... `Alt`+`I`, `↕`
and enter/select desired hanging-indent position.

> *To remove hanging indent altogether, type 0 (zero).*

7 Click OK .... `Enter`

CUSTOMIZE NUMBERED LIST

1 Click **Format** .... `Alt`+`O`

2 Click **Bullets and Numbering** .... `N`

3 Click **Numbered** tab, if necessary.............. `Alt`+`N`

4 Click number/letter format to customize, if necessary.

5 Click Customize... .... `Alt`+`T`

Click to change font for selected number/letter format.

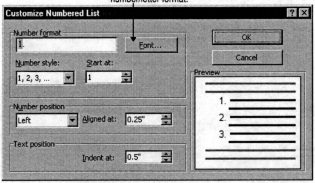

6 Click **Number style** drop-down arrow and select desired number/letter style.

7 Click **Start at** increment box .... `Tab`, `↑↓`
   and enter/select desired starting number.

   To modify *Number position*:

   a Click **Number position** drop-down arrow and select desired text alignment.

   b Click **Aligned at** increment box .... `Tab`, `↑↓`
     and enter/select desired number/letter position.

   📖 *To remove number/letter indent altogether, type* 0 *(zero).*

   To modify *Text position*:

   Click **Indent at** increment box .... `Alt`+`I`, `↑↓`
   and enter/select desired hanging-indent position.

   📖 *To remove hanging indent altogether, type* 0 *(zero).*

8 Click 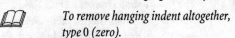 .... `Enter`

EDIT/FORMAT TEXT

Insert Multilevel List

If a single paragraph formatted with a heading-level style is selected in step 1, below, this option is unavailable.

1 Select text to format as a multilevel list.

2 Click **F̲ormat** .... **Alt**+**O**

3 Click **Bullets and N̲umbering** .... **N**

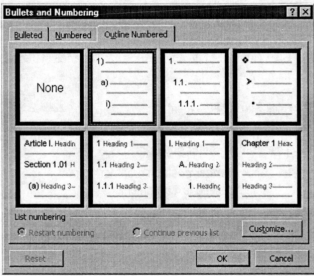

4 Click **O̲utline Numbered** tab .... **Alt**+**U**
   if necessary.

5 Click desired multilevel format from palette.

> 📖 *The **None** option removes all bullet and numbering options selected in the Bullets and Numbering dialog box, including those on other tabs.*

6 Click **OK** .... **Enter**
   to apply selected multilevel list format.

CUSTOMIZE MULTILEVEL LIST

1   Click **Format**.. `Alt`+`O`

2   Click **Bullets and Numbering** .... `N`

3   Click **Outline Numbered** tab....................... `Alt`+`U`
    if necessary.

4   Click multilevel format to customize, if necessary.

5   Click `Customize...` .... `Alt`+`T`

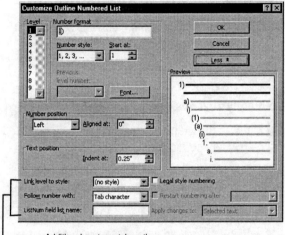

Additional custom style options

6   Click **Level** list box and select level to change.

7   Click **Number style** drop-down arrow and select desired
    bullet/number style.

8   Click **Start at** increment box and enter/select starting
    number or letter.

9   Click **Previous level number** drop-down arrow and
    select number formatting from previous levels that you
    want to include with subordinate levels.

>   *The above option is unavailable if level 1
> was selected in step 6.*

continued...

EDIT/FORMAT TEXT

CUSTOMIZE MULTILEVEL LIST (CONT.)

To change font for selected multilevel list format:

a Click ⬚ Font... ⬚ .... **Alt** + **F**

b Select desired font, style, and point size.

c Click ⬚ OK ⬚ .... **Enter**

To modify *Number position*:

a Click **Number position** drop-down arrow and enter/select desired text alignment.

b Click **Aligned at** increment box and select/enter desired number/letter position.

> 📖 *To remove number/letter indent altogether, type* 0 *(zero).*

To modify *Text position*:

Click **Indent at** increment box and enter/select desired hanging indent position.

> 📖 *To remove hanging indent altogether, type* 0 *(zero).*

To access more custom style options:

> 📖 *The illustration on the previous page displays the additional custom style options.*

Click ⬚ More ⬇ ⬚ .... **Alt** + **M**

10 Repeat steps 6–9 to change formatting for additional levels.

11 Click ⬚ OK ⬚ .... **Enter**
to apply customized multilevel list format.

EDIT/FORMAT TEXT

CHARACTER FORMATTING

Change Font

LETTER CASE

COMMAND	SHORTCUT
Switch letter case	Shift + F3
All caps	Ctrl + Shift + A
Small caps	Ctrl + Shift + K

FONT

TOOLBAR BUTTON/COMMAND	SHORTCUT
Font Times New Roman	Ctrl + Shift + F
Access Symbol font set	Ctrl + Shift + Q

FONT SIZE

TOOLBAR BUTTON/COMMAND	SHORTCUT
Font Size 10	Ctrl + Shift + P
Increase one point size	Ctrl +]
Decrease one point size	Ctrl + [
Increase to next point size	Ctrl + Shift + .
Decrease to next point size	Ctrl + Shift + ,

EDIT/FORMAT TEXT

FONT STYLE

TOOLBAR BUTTON/COMMAND	SHORTCUT
Return to default font	**Ctrl** + **Shift** + **Z**
Bold **B**	**Ctrl** + **B**
Italic **I**	**Ctrl** + **I**
Underline **U**	**Ctrl** + **U**
Underline, words only—not spaces	**Ctrl** + **Shift** + **W**
Double underline	**Ctrl** + **Shift** + **D**
Superscript	**Ctrl** + **Shift** + **=**
Subscript	**Ctrl** + **=**

ON-SCREEN VIEWING

TOOLBAR BUTTON/COMMAND	SHORTCUT
Show/Hide ¶ **¶**	**Ctrl** + **Shift** + **8**
Display hidden text	**Ctrl** + **Shift** + **H**

Change Letter Case

You can also cycle through case options for selected text by pressing Shift+F3 repeatedly until selected text is shown as desired.

1   Select text with case(s) to change.

2   Click **Format**, **Change Case**................ **Alt** + **O**, **E**

3   Select desired letter case option:

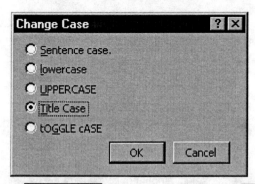

4 Click OK .... Enter

DROP CAP

*To remove the drop cap from selected text, complete steps 1-3
below, then skip to step 5; the options in step 4 are unavailable.*

1 Select letter or text you want to format as drop cap.

2 Click **Format**, **Drop Cap** .... Alt + O, D

3 Select desired drop cap **Position:**

continued…

EDIT/FORMAT TEXT

DROP CAP (CONT.)

4   Set any desired **Options**:

-   Click **Font** drop-down arrow and select font
    to use for drop cap.

-   Click **Lines to drop** increment box and enter/select
    number of lines to extend drop cap downward in
    paragraph text.

-   Click **Distance from text** increment box and
    enter/select amount of space to place between drop
    cap and paragraph text.

5   Click  .... Enter

Change Font Using Menu

Choices below vary with the selected font. To set custom
*superscript and subscript positions, see **Change Character***
***Spacing**, page 77, adjust character position option.*

1   Select text with font to change.

2   Click **Format**, **Font**....................................

3   Click **Font** tab, if necessary..........................

4   Select desired options:

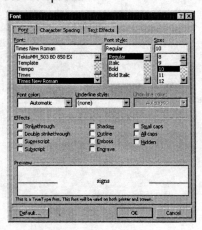

EDIT/FORMAT TEXT

To use selected options as default settings:

*This change affects all new documents based on the current template (e.g., NORMAL.DOT). Further, clicking the **Default** button here changes the default settings for all options selected in the **Font** dialog box, including those on other tabs.*

a Click `Default...` .... `Alt`+`D`

b Click `Yes` .... `Enter`
when confirmation dialog box appears.

5 Click `OK` .... `Enter`

Change Character Spacing

1 Select text with formatting to change.

2 Click **Format**, **Font** .... `Ctrl`+`D`

3 Click **Character Spacing** tab .... `Alt`+`R`
if necessary.

4 Enter/select desired **Scale** .... `Tab`, `↑↓`, `Enter`
percentage, if necessary.

5 Click **Spacing** drop-down .... `Tab`, `↑↓`, `Enter`
arrow and select desired spacing option
(**Normal**, **Expanded**, or **Condensed**).

6 Click **By** increment box .... `Tab`, `↑↓`
and enter/select distance
to place between characters.

continued...

EDIT/FORMAT TEXT

CHANGE CHARACTER SPACING (CONT.)

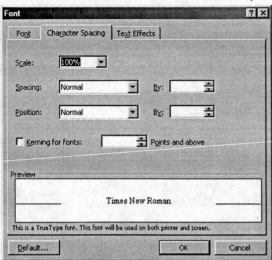

To adjust character position:

a Click **Position** .... `Alt`+`P`, `↕`, `Enter`
drop-down arrow and select desired position in
relation to baseline (**Normal**, **Raised**, or **Lowered**).

b Click **By** increment box .... `Alt`+`Y`, `↕`
and type number of points to raise/lower
text in relation to baseline, if necessary.

To adjust kerning automatically:

*Kerning is only available for TrueType or Adobe Type
Manager fonts.*

a Select **Kerning for fonts** check box..... `Alt`+`K`

b Click **Points and above** .... `Tab`, `↕`
increment box and enter/select desired point size.

7 Click OK .... `Enter`

EDIT/FORMAT TEXT

Format Painter

*Format Painter copies the applied character style and formatting of the first character of selected text. If a paragraph mark is selected, Word copies the paragraph style in addition to the character style. (See **Styles**, page 110, for more information.)*

1 Select text containing character formatting to copy.

2 Click **Format Painter** 🖌 .... `Ctrl`+`Shift`+`C`
on **Standard** toolbar to copy formatting
of selected text to a single location.

OR

Double–click **Format Painter** 🖌 to copy formatting
to multiple locations.

The arrow pointer changes to: 🖌I

3 Select text to copy character formatting to.

4 Press **Shift+Ctrl+V**........................ `Ctrl`+`Shift`+`V`
if you used the shortcut key method in step 2.

If you double–clicked Format Painter button in step 2:

a Repeat step 3 to copy character formatting to
additional locations.

b Deselect **Format Painter** 🖌 .... `Esc`
to turn off Format Painter.

EDIT/FORMAT TEXT

Insert Symbol or Special Character

Symbols and *special characters* are characters that are not available on the keyboard, such as bullets, European letters, or trademark symbols.

INSERT SYMBOL

1   Place cursor where you want to insert symbol.

2   Click **Insert**, **Symbol**.......................... `Alt` + `I`, `S`

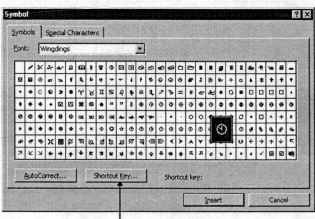

Click to assign shortcut key to symbol.

3   Click **Symbols** tab, if necessary .... `S`

4   Click **Font** drop-down arrow.......... `Tab`, `↕`, `Enter`
    and select font set containing symbol to insert.

> 📖   *Clicking once on a symbol magnifies it for easier viewing.*

5   Double–click desired symbol......... `Tab`, `↔`, `Enter`

6   Click [Close] .... `Enter`

EDIT/FORMAT TEXT

INSERT SPECIAL CHARACTER

1 Place cursor where you want to insert special character.

2 Click **Insert**, **Symbol** .... Alt + I , S

3 Click **Special Characters** tab .... Alt + P
if necessary.

4 Double-click desired special **Character** .. ⬍ , Enter

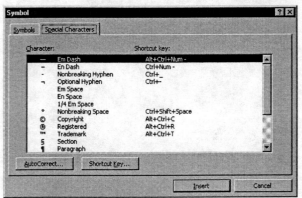

5 Click   Close   .... Enter

EDIT/FORMAT TEXT

EDITING OPTIONS

1 Click **Tools**, **Options** .... Alt + T , O

2 Click **Edit** tab, if necessary...................... Ctrl + Tab

3 Select/deselect **Editing options** as desired:

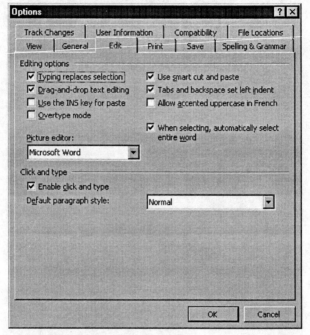

Choices vary depending upon installed applications.

4 Click [OK] .... Enter

EDIT/FORMAT TEXT

FIELDS

Fields are placeholders for text that may change during editing, such as page numbers, dates, and time fields. The text in a field can be updated automatically.

Insert Date and Time

1   Place cursor in document where you want to insert current day, date, and/or time.

2   Click **Insert**, **Date and Time** .... Alt + I , T

Click to set selected format as default.

3   Select desired day, date, and/or time format from **Available formats** list box.

    To convert selected format to field:

    Select **Update automatically** .... Alt + U
    check box to update the day, date, and/or time periodically.

    *See **Update Field Code/Result**, page 85, for more information.*

4   Click  OK .... Enter

EDIT/FORMAT TEXT

Insert Field

1   Place cursor where you want to insert a field.

2   Click **Insert**, **Field** .... `Alt`+`I`,`F`

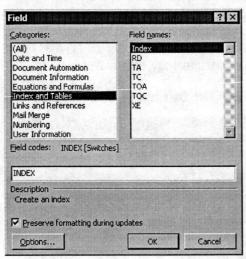

3   Select desired field **Categories** ....

4   Click **Field names** list box.......................... `Tab`,
and select field to insert.

To add specific element/instruction to field:

This function is not available for certain **Numbering** *and* **Equations and Formulas** *fields.*

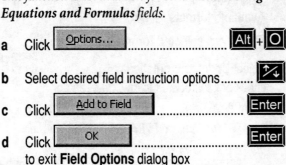

a   Click [Options...] .... `Alt`+`O`

b   Select desired field instruction options..........

c   Click [Add to Field] .... `Enter`

d   Click [OK] .... `Enter`
to exit **Field Options** dialog box
and return to **Field** dialog box.

To update character formatting automatically:

*This function is disabled by default. It is not available for certain **Numbering** and **Equations and Formulas** fields.*

Deselect **P**reserve formatting during updates....
check box.

5 Click  .... Enter

View Field Code/Result

1 Select field for which you want to switch display to codes or results.

2 Point at field and right-click.

3 Click **T**oggle Field Codes/Results ....

Update Field Code/Result

1 Select field to update.

2 Press **F9** ....

OR

1 Right-click field to update.

2 Click **U**pdate Field ....

EDIT/FORMAT TEXT

HEADERS/FOOTERS

For information on creating a different header and footer for just the first page of a section, or different odd- and even-numbered page headers and footers, see the advanced header/footer option in the procedure below. Also see page 88, for information on changing the distance headers and footers print from the edge of the page.

Create Header/Footer

1   Click **View**, **Header and Footer**........... Alt + V , H

To create footer:

Click **Switch Between Header and Footer** 🔁
to move to the **Footer** box.

2   Type desired text in **Header** box .... *text*
OR

Type desired text in **Footer** box .... *text*
OR

Click [Insert AutoText ▾] and select AutoText item
to insert.

OR

Insert desired fields using **Header and Footer**
toolbar buttons.

EDIT/FORMAT TEXT

TOOLBAR BUTTON	DESCRIPTION
Insert Page Number	Inserts a PAGE field at the location of the cursor.
Insert Number of Pages	Inserts the total number of pages in document.
Format Page Number	Displays formatting options for Number, Chapter, or Page Numbering. *(See **Insert Page Numbers**, page 89.)*
Insert Date	Inserts DATE field at cursor location.
Insert Time	Inserts TIME field at cursor location.

To create advanced header/footer:

a   Click **Page Setup** 📖 on **Header and Footer** toolbar.

b   Click **Layout** tab, if necessary .... **Alt** + **L**

c   Select desired **Headers and footers** check box option:

    ■ **Different odd and even** .... **Alt** + **O**
       Creates one header (or footer) for even–numbered pages and another for odd–numbered pages.

    ■ **Different first page** .... **Alt** + **F**
       Creates a different header (or footer) for the first page of a section or document.

d   Click   OK   .... **Enter**

3   Click **Close** .... **Alt** + **C**

EDIT/FORMAT TEXT

Edit Header/Footer

You can double-click a dimmed header or footer to access the Header or Footer box quickly.

1   Click **View**, **Header and Footer**............ `Alt`+`V`, `H`

2   Locate header/footer to edit:

    - Click **Switch Between Header and Footer** 🖺
      as necessary.

    - Click **Show Previous** 🖺 to move to previous
      header or footer.

    - Click **Show Next** 🖺 to move to next header
      or footer.

3   Edit header or footer text as desired.

4   Click Close .... `Alt`+`C`

Header/Footer Placement

*If the setting in the **Header** increment box is greater than the amount in the **Top** increment box, Word 2000 pushes the body text downward. Similarly, if the increment setting is less than the amount in the **Top** increment box, the body text is given that much more room on the page.*

☞ *WITH RULERS DISPLAYED*

1   Double-click on dark gray area............ `Alt`+`F`, `U`
    of horizontal ruler or anywhere on vertical ruler.

    📖   *The vertical ruler is only available in Print
          Layout view and Print Preview.*

2   Click **Margins** tab, if necessary................. `Alt`+`M`

3   Click increment box of each margin to change and
    enter/select desired margin space **From edge**:

EDIT/FORMAT TEXT

- **He_a_der** .... Alt + A, ⇙

- **Footer:** .... Alt + . , ⇙

4   Click **Apply to** drop-down arrow and select **Whole document**.

5   Click [OK] .... Enter

Insert Page Numbers

*For bound documents, two additional options are available in the **Alignment** drop-down list: **Inside** and **Outside**. These options place page numbers on the inner or outer margins of facing pages (see Preview box in illustration below).*

1   Click **Insert**, **Page Numbers** .... Alt + I, U

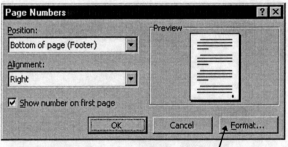

Click to change page-numbering format.

2   Select desired page number **Position**.

3   Click **Alignment** drop-down arrow and select desired page number alignment.

   To suppress page numbers on first page:

   Deselect **Show number on first page** .... Alt + S
   check box, if necessary.

4   Click [OK] .... Enter
   to close **Page Numbers** dialog box.

EDIT/FORMAT TEXT

MACROS

*A **macro** is an automated combination of sequential commands. To create a macro, you let Word 2000 "record" the steps involved in your task. Then, let the macro "run" each time you want the task performed.*

*You can make a macro available to all documents or only to those based on a particular template. Also, you can create a toolbar button or assign a keyboard shortcut to a macro, making the macro more readily accessible. (See **Organizer**, page 117, for more information.)*

Record (Create) Macro

1   Click **T**ools, **M**acro ....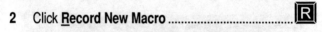

2   Click **R**ecord New Macro .... R

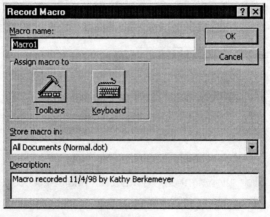

3   Type new **M**acro name .... *name*

4   Verify location to **S**tore macro in. Change macro location, if necessary, using drop-down arrow.

   The new macro is stored in the global template, NORMAL.DOT, by default and is available to All Documents.

5   Verify macro **D**escription. Make any changes as necessary in text box.

To create toolbar button for macro:

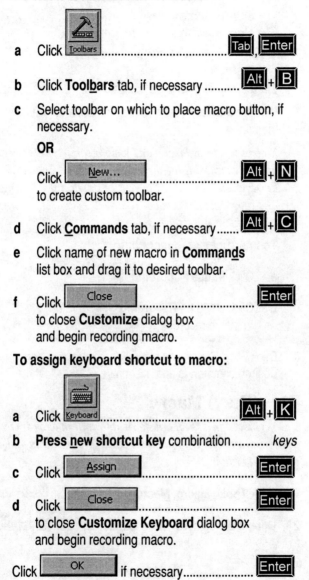

a Click `Toolbars` .... Tab, Enter

b Click **Toolbars** tab, if necessary .... Alt + B

c Select toolbar on which to place macro button, if necessary.

OR

Click `New...` .... Alt + N
to create custom toolbar.

d Click **Commands** tab, if necessary .... Alt + C

e Click name of new macro in **Commands** list box and drag it to desired toolbar.

f Click `Close` .... Enter
to close **Customize** dialog box and begin recording macro.

To assign keyboard shortcut to macro:

a Click `Keyboard` .... Alt + K

b **Press new shortcut key** combination .... *keys*

c Click `Assign` .... Enter

d Click `Close` .... Enter
to close **Customize Keyboard** dialog box and begin recording macro.

6 Click `OK` if necessary .... Enter

continued...

EDIT/FORMAT TEXT

RECORD (CREATE) MACRO (CONT.)

*The **Record Macro** dialog box closes.
The **Macro** toolbar appears, indicating
that you can begin recording your macro:*

The arrow pointer changes to:

7 Perform desired sequence of commands to include in the macro.

Macros will record menu and toolbar commands as well as options executed using the mouse. Mouse movements, however, such as moving the cursor or selecting, moving, and copying text, cannot be recorded. You must perform these actions using the keyboard.

To interrupt macro recording:

a Click **Pause Recording** II●

b Click **Resume Recording** II● to return to macro recording.

8 Click **Stop Recording** ■ when finished performing desired commands and actions.

Run (Play) Macro

Unless you assign a keyboard shortcut to your macro (or create a toolbar button for it), you must use this procedure any time you wish to run it.

1 Click **T**ools, **M**acro, **M**acros........................ **Alt**+**F8**

2 Double-click **M**acro name to run............. ⬆⬇, **Enter**

EDIT/FORMAT TEXT

NEWSPAPER–STYLE COLUMNS

Create Newspaper Columns Using Mouse

*To create custom columns using mouse, see **Set Margins Using Ruler**, page 98.*

1   Select text (or section of column) to/from which you want to add/remove newspaper–style columns.

> 📖   *Newspaper–style columns are section–specific. Section breaks are inserted above and below any selected text.*

2   Click **Columns** on **Standard** toolbar.

3   Drag arrow pointer over drop-down column number palette to locate desired column layout. Click to select desired column layout.

OR

Click [1 Column] to return document to regular text layout, one "column" that is 6.5" wide.

Create Newspaper Columns Using Menu

While you can create newspaper columns in all views in Word 2000, your document will be moved into Print Layout view so that you may view the change if you create columns in Normal view, Web Layout view, or Outline view.

1   Select text (or section of column) to/from which you want to add/remove newspaper–style columns.

2   Click **Format**, **Columns** .... Alt + O , C

continued...

EDIT/FORMAT TEXT

CREATE NEWSPAPER COLUMNS USING MENU (CONT.)

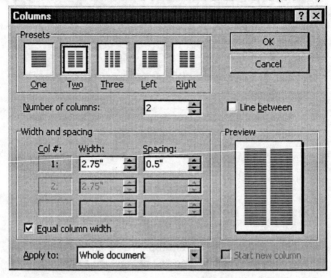

3 Select desired column format option from **Presets**.

   OR

   Click **Number of columns**.............. Alt + N , ⬆⬇
   increment box and enter/select
   number of columns to insert (0-13).

4 Click [OK] .... Enter

Create Custom Columns

*See also **Set Margins Using Ruler**, page 98.*

1 Select text (or section of column) to/from which you
   want to add/remove newspaper–style columns.

2 Click **Format**, **Columns** .... Alt + O , C

3 Deselect **Equal column width** check box ... Alt + E

4 Click **Width** increment box for column to modify and
   enter/select new width measurement.

EDIT/FORMAT TEXT

5   Click **Spacing** increment box for column to modify and enter/select new spacing measurement.

6   Navigate through **Width** and **Spacing** increment boxes, as necessary, to set desired column proportions:

- Move forward... `Tab`

- Move backward .... `Shift` + `Tab`

7   Click [OK] .... `Enter`

Force the Start of New Newspaper Column

1   Place cursor where you wish to insert column break.

2   Click **Insert**, **Break** .... `Alt` + `I`, `B`

3   Select **Column break** radio button....................... `C`

   Text after cursor moves to the top of the next column.

4   Click [OK] .... `Enter`

EDIT/FORMAT TEXT

PAGE AND SECTION FORMATTING

Insert Breaks

*You can divide pages in a document into sections. A **section** is a portion of your document that is formatted differently from other sections of the document. Until a new section break is inserted, Word treats the entire document as a single section.*

INSERT BREAKS USING KEYBOARD

BREAK TYPE	SHORTCUT
Line break	**Shift** + **Enter**
Page break	**Ctrl** + **Enter**
Column break	**Ctrl** + **Shift** + **Enter**

INSERT BREAKS USING MENU

*You can also insert column breaks with the **Format, Columns** command. (See **Newspaper–Style Columns**, page 93.)*

1 Place cursor where you want to insert break.

2 Click **I**nsert, **B**reak.................... **Alt** + **I**, **B**

EDIT/FORMAT TEXT

3 Select from available **Break types**.

4 Select from available **Section break types**:

- **Next page** inserts a section break at the bottom of the current page; new section starts at the top of the next page.

- **Continuous** inserts a section break on the current page without inserting a page break; new section starts immediately below previous section.

- **Even page** inserts a section break; new section starts on next even–numbered page.

- **Odd page** inserts a section break; new section starts on next odd–numbered page.

5 Click  .... Enter

EDIT/FORMAT TEXT

PAGE SETUP

Margins

SET MARGINS USING RULER

Changes page margins in Web Layout view, Print Layout view, or Print Preview, although the vertical ruler is only available in Print Layout view and Print Preview.

This feature is also available when working with newspaper-style columns. Note, however, that newspaper columns will remain of equal width no matter which column marker you move unless the **Equal column width** *check box is first deselected in the* **Columns** *dialog box. See* **Create Custom Columns**, *page 94. When this option is deselected, the following symbol appears on the dark gray part of the horizontal ruler:* 🔲

⟲ ON HORIZONTAL OR VERTICAL RULER

1   Position arrow pointer over margin boundary to change.
    OR
    Position arrow pointer over column marker to adjust newspaper column margin.

    The arrow pointer changes to a sizing arrow: ↔
    ScreenTips appear, indicating which margin boundary (or column marker) you are moving: Left Margin, Right Margin, Top Margin, or Bottom Margin.

2   Click and hold down left mouse button.

3   Drag selected margin to new position.

4   Release mouse button.

EDIT/FORMAT TEXT

SET MARGINS USING MENU

✍ WITH RULERS DISPLAYED

1 Select text with margins to change.

2 Double–click on dark gray area .... **Alt** + **F** , **U**
of horizontal ruler or anywhere on vertical ruler.

> 📖 *The vertical ruler is only available in Print
> Layout view and Print Preview.*

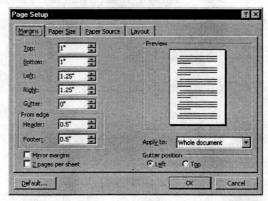

3 Click **Margins** tab, if necessary .... **Alt** + **M**

4 Click increment box of each margin to change
and enter/select desired margin space.

To change default margin settings:

*This change affects all new documents based on the
current template (e.g., NORMAL.DOT). Further, clicking the
Default button here changes the default settings for all
options selected in the **Page Setup** dialog box, including
those on other tabs.*

a Click [Default...] .... **Alt** + **D**

b Click [Yes] .... **Enter**
when confirmation dialog box appears.

5 Click [OK] .... **Enter**

EDIT/FORMAT TEXT

ADJUST MARGINS FOR BOUND DOCUMENTS

*See **Header/Footer Placement**, page 88.*

*To create different headers and/or footers for odd and even pages, refer to the advanced header/footer option, **Create Header/Footer**, page 86.*

☞ WITH RULERS DISPLAYED

1 Double–click on dark gray area .... `Alt`+`F`,`U`
of horizontal ruler or anywhere on vertical ruler.

> 📖 *The vertical ruler is only available in Print Layout view and Print Preview.*

2 Click **Margins** tab, if necessary .... `Alt`+`M`

3 Select **Mirror Margins** check box .... `Alt`+`I`

4 Click **Inside** increment box and enter/select desired margin space for bound edges.

5 Click **Outside** increment box and enter/select desired margin space for outer edges.

6 Click **Apply to** drop-down arrow and select **Whole document.**

7 Click `    OK    ` .... `Enter`

PAPER SIZE AND PAGE ORIENTATION

☞ WITH RULERS DISPLAYED

1 Select page(s) with size and orientation to change.

2 Double–click on dark gray area .... `Alt`+`F`,`U`
of horizontal ruler or anywhere on vertical ruler.

> 📖 *The vertical ruler is only available in Print Layout view and Print Preview.*

3 Click **Paper Size** tab, if necessary .... `Alt`+`S`

4 Click **Paper size** drop-down arrow and select desired paper size.

> 📖 *Choices depend on selected printer.*

To select custom paper size:

a Click **Width** increment box and enter/select desired paper width.

> 📖 *Setting paper width and height dimensions changes the **Paper size** drop-down list box setting to **Custom size** automatically.*

b Click **Height** increment box and enter/select desired paper height.

5 Select desired **Orientation** radio button option:

- **Portrait** .... Alt + I

- **Landscape** .... Alt + C

6 Click **Apply to** drop-down arrow and select desired option, if necessary.

> 📖 *Choices vary depending upon text selected in step 1.*

7 Click OK .... Enter

EDIT/FORMAT TEXT

PAPER SOURCE

☞ WITH RULERS DISPLAYED

1   Select page(s) with paper source to change.

2   Double–click on dark gray area............ **Alt**+**F**,**U**
    of horizontal ruler or anywhere on vertical ruler.

> 📖 *The vertical ruler is only available in Print Layout view and Print Preview.*

3   Click **Paper Source** tab, if necessary .... **Alt**+**P**

4   Click **First page** list box and select paper source for first page.

5   Click **Other pages** list box and select paper source for pages other than the first, if necessary.

6   Click **Apply to** drop-down arrow and select desired option, if necessary.

> 📖 *Choices vary depending upon text selected in step 1.*

To change default paper source:

This change affects all new documents based on the current template (e.g., NORMAL.DOT). Further, clicking the Default button here changes the default settings for all options selected in the Page Setup dialog box, including those on other tabs.

a   Click [Default...] .... **Alt**+**D**

b   Click [Yes] .... **Enter**
    when confirmation dialog box appears.

7   Click [OK] .... **Enter**

PAGE LAYOUT

1 Select pages with layout to change.

2 Double–click on dark gray area .... 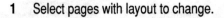 of horizontal ruler or anywhere on vertical ruler.

> 📖 *The vertical ruler is only available in Print*
> *Layout view and Print Preview.*

3 Click **Layout** tab, if necessary .... Alt + L

4 Click **Section start** drop-down arrow and select start point for current section.

5 Click **Vertical alignment** drop-down arrow and select desired vertical text alignment (**Top**, **Center**, **Justified**, or **Bottom**).

6 Click **Apply to** drop-down arrow and select desired option, if necessary.

7 Click 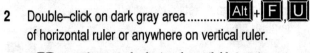 .... Enter

> 📖 *Choices vary depending upon text selected*
> *in step 1.*

ADD LINE NUMBERS TO SELECTED TEXT

Line numbers appear only in Print Preview and on the printed
document.

1 Select text to number by line.

2 Click **File**, **Page Setup** .... Alt + F , U

3 Click **Layout** tab, if necessary .... Alt + L

4 Click 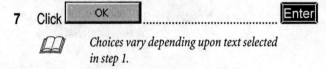 .... Alt + N

5 Select **Add line numbering** check box L

continued...

ADD LINE NUMBERS TO SELECTED TEXT (CONT.)

6 Click **Start at** increment box....................... `Tab`, `↑↓`
  and enter/select first line to include
  in numbered sequence.

7 Click **From text** increment box.................... `Tab`, `↑↓`
  and enter/select distance between
  line numbers and document text, if necessary.

8 Click **Count by** increment box .... `Tab`, `↑↓`
  and enter/select increment to number
  lines by (e.g., 2, 5, 10).

9 Select desired **Numbering** radio button option:

■ **Restart each page**	Restarts line numbering (with the number shown in the **Start at** increment box) on each new page.
■ **Restart each section**	Restarts line numbering (with the number shown in the **Start at** increment box) at the beginning of each new section.
■ **Continuous**	Continues a single line-numbering sequence throughout portion of document selected in step 1.

10 Click [OK] twice .... `Enter`, `Enter`

EDIT/FORMAT TEXT

PARAGRAPH FORMATTING

Format Indents and Spacing

PARAGRAPH ALIGNMENT

TOOLBAR BUTTON	SHORTCUT
Left Align (default)	Ctrl + L
Center Align	Ctrl + E
Right Align	Ctrl + R
Justify	Ctrl + J

INDENTS AND SPACING

TOOLBAR BUTTON/COMMAND	SHORTCUT
Hanging indent	Ctrl + T
Remove hanging indent	Shift + Ctrl + T
Left indent	Ctrl + M
Remove left indent	Shift + Ctrl + M
Decrease Indent	*n/a*
Increase Indent	*n/a*
Open/Remove one line before	Ctrl + 0 (zero)
Single spacing	Ctrl + 1
One–and–a–half line spacing	Ctrl + 5
Double spacing	Ctrl + 2

EDIT/FORMAT TEXT

FORMAT PARAGRAPH INDENTS USING RULER

In Word 2000, ScreenTips appear when you position the arrow pointer on an indent marker.

✑ WITH RULER DISPLAYED

1 Select paragraph(s) with indents to change.

2 Place arrow pointer on top of desired indent marker:

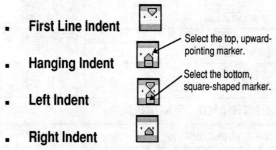

- **First Line Indent**

  Select the top, upward-pointing marker.

- **Hanging Indent**

  Select the bottom, square-shaped marker.

- **Left Indent**

- **Right Indent**

3 Click and hold down mouse button while dragging indent marker to desired position.

4 Release mouse button.

OR

1 Select paragraph(s) with indents to change.

2 Click tab type button 🔲 (default) on left end of horizontal ruler until either of the following appear:

- **First Line Indent** ▽
- **Hanging Indent** ⬜

3 Place arrow pointer on horizontal ruler where you wish to insert first-line indent or hanging indent.

4 Click mouse button.

To move indent:

Click horizontal ruler again in desired indent position.

EDIT/FORMAT TEXT

FORMAT PARAGRAPH INDENTS AND SPACING USING MENU

1 Select paragraph(s) to format.

2 Click **Format**, **Paragraph** .... **Alt** + **O**, **P**

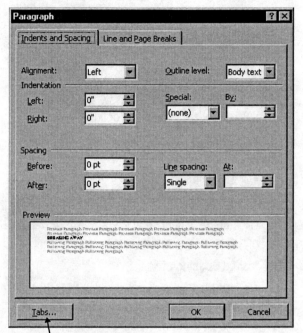

Set tabs for selected paragraphs.

3 Click **Indents and Spacing** tab .... **Alt** + **I**
if necessary.

4 Click **Alignment** drop-down arrow and select desired paragraph alignment.

To assign outline levels to selected text:

Click **Outline level** drop-down arrow and select desired outline level to assign.

continued...

EDIT/FORMAT TEXT

FORMAT PARAGRAPH INDENTS... (CONT.)

5   Set desired **Indentation** option:

- Click **Left** increment box and enter/select distance to place between left margin and selected paragraph.

- Click **Right** increment box and enter/select distance to place between right margin and selected paragraph.

OR

a   Click **Special** drop-down arrow and select desired special indentation option:

- **First line**   Indents only the first line of paragraph.

- **Hanging**   Indents all lines in a paragraph except the first.

b   Click **By** increment box .... Tab , ↗↓
and enter/select special indent width.

6   Set desired **Spacing** option:

- Click **Before** increment box and enter/select distance to place between selected paragraph and text above it.

- Click **After** increment box and enter/select distance to place between selected paragraph and text below it.

OR

a   Click **Line spacing** drop-down arrow and select desired line spacing option.

b   Click **At** increment box (if you selected **At Least**, **Exactly**, or **Multiple** in the step above) and enter/select distance to place between lines within selected paragraph.

7   Click   OK   .... Enter

EDIT/FORMAT TEXT

Text Flow

1 Select paragraph(s) to format.

2 Click **Format, Paragraph** .... **Alt**+**O**, **P**

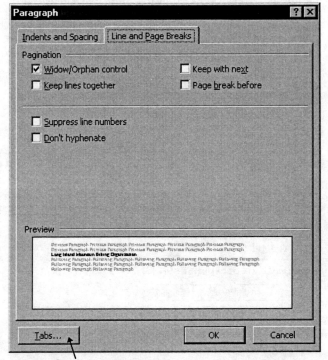

Set tabs for selected paragraphs.

3 Click **Line and Page Breaks** tab .... **Alt**+**P**
   if necessary.

4 Select desired check box options.

5 Click ▢ OK .... **Enter**

EDIT/FORMAT TEXT

STYLES

Styles group a series of formatting elements into one function, which can then be saved within a template or as part of a document. They can also be copied between different templates and documents using the Organizer (see page 117).

*A drop-down palette of available styles is on the **Formatting** toolbar; simply click the **Style** drop-down arrow.*

*There are two basic style types: **paragraph** and **character**. These two style types are denoted differently on the drop-down palette and in the **Style** dialog box styles gallery.*

STYLE TYPE	GALLERY	DROP-DOWN PALETTE
paragraph	¶	≡ ¶ 10 pt
character	a	≡ a
default	▶	n/a

STYLE GALLERY DEFAULT SETTINGS:

- ▶ a Default Paragraph Font

- ▶ ¶ Normal

Apply Style

APPLY STYLE USING TOOLBAR

1   Select paragraph(s) or character(s) to
    which you want to apply style.

2   Click **Style** [Normal ▼] .... Ctrl + Shift + S
    on **Formatting** toolbar.

3   Click style to apply................................ ↑↓, Enter
    on drop–down style palette.

EDIT/FORMAT TEXT

APPLY STYLE USING MENU

1 Select paragraph(s) or character(s) to
which you want to apply style.

2 Click **Format**, **Style** .... Alt + O, S

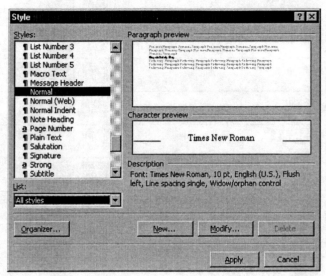

3 Select **Styles** to apply ....

To access more styles:

Click **List** drop-down arrow .... Tab, ↑↓, Enter
and select from the following options:

- **Styles in use**

- **All styles** (default)

- **User-defined styles**

4 Click  Apply .... Alt + A

EDIT/FORMAT TEXT

APPLY STYLE USING KEYBOARD

COMMAND/STYLE	SHORTCUT
Normal	Ctrl + Shift + N
Remove character style(s)	Ctrl + Space
Remove paragraph formatting	Ctrl + Q
Current style	Ctrl + Shift + S
Heading 1	Ctrl + Alt + 1
Heading 2	Ctrl + Alt + 2
Heading 3	Ctrl + Alt + 3
List bullet	Ctrl + Shift + L
AutoFormat	Ctrl + Alt + K

Create Style

1   Format paragraph, text, or item to base style on.

2   Select formatted paragraph, text, or item.

3   Click **Format**, **Style**.............................. Alt + O, S

4   Click **New...** .... Alt + N

Click to assign shortcut key to style.

5 Type new style **Name** .... *name*

6 Verify or change the following list box settings:

- **Style type**

  Two basic style types, **Paragraph** (default) and **Character**.

- **Based on**

  Select style on which to base new one. New paragraph styles are based on the style applied to the active paragraph.

- **Style for following paragraph**

  Select style to apply to following paragraphs, if desired. This option is not available if **Character** was selected for the first option above.

continued...

7   Select advanced style check box options, if desired:

- **A̲dd to template** .... **Alt**+**A**
  Adds style to current template.

- **A̲utomatically update** .... **Alt**+**U**
  Modifies style each time you apply manual
  formatting to a paragraph formatted in
  selected style.

8   Click [OK] .... **Enter**
  to create style and close **New Style** dialog box.

9   Click [Apply] .... **Esc**
  to close **Style** dialog box and apply new style.

EDIT/FORMAT TEXT

Modify Style

MODIFY STYLE USING TOOLBAR

1　Make desired formatting changes to existing text containing style to modify.

2　Select formatted text.

3　Click Style `Normal ▼` .... `Ctrl`+`Shift`+`S`
on **Formatting** toolbar.

4　Select style to modify.............................. `↑↓`, `Enter`

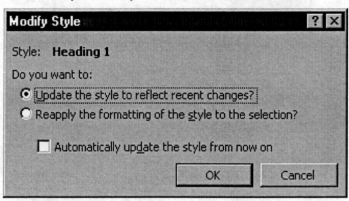

*The name of the selected **Style** appears at the top of the dialog box.*

5　Select **Update the style to reflect recent changes** radio button, if necessary.

6　Click  .... `Enter`

EDIT/FORMAT TEXT

MODIFY STYLE USING MENU

1 Select paragraph, text, or item with style to modify.

2 Click **Format**, **Style**............................... `Alt`+`O`, `S`

*The **Style** dialog box appears. The name of the style applied to the selected text is highlighted in the **Styles** list box.*

3 Click [Modify...] .... `Alt`+`M`

4 Click [Format ▼] .... `Alt`+`O`

and select style element to modify from pop-up menu.

5 Set formatting for selected style element as desired.

6 Repeat steps 4 and 5 as necessary.

7 Click [OK] .... `Enter`

DELETE STYLE

This procedure can be undone using the Undo procedure.

Built–in styles, such as heading level styles, cannot be deleted.

1 Select paragraph, text, or item with style to delete.

2 Click **Format**, **Style**............................... `Alt`+`O`, `S`

3 Verify style to delete in **Styles** list box.

4 Click [Delete] .... `Alt`+`D`

5 Click [Yes] .... `Enter`
to confirm style deletion.

6 Click [Close] .... `Esc`

EDIT/FORMAT TEXT

Organizer

The Organizer displays, copies, deletes, and renames styles, AutoText, toolbars, and macros attached to documents or templates.

1 Click **Tools, Templates and Add-Ins..** 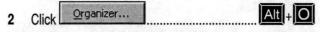 `Alt`+`T`,`I`

2 Click **Organizer...** .... `Alt`+`O`

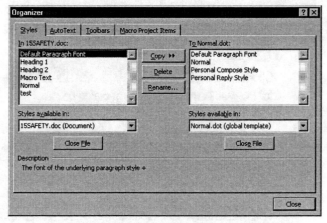

*The **Organizer** dialog box contains four tabs: Styles, AutoText, Toolbars, and Macros Project Items. The available commands in each of the tabs are identical.*

*The [item] **available in** drop-down list box on the left side of the dialog box defaults to the current document or template; the [item] **available in** drop-down list box on the right side defaults to NORMAL.DOT (**global template**). The list box names switch between **To [template]** and **In [template]**, depending on which list box has items selected.*

3 Click named tab containing elements to modify.

To display/open a different document or template:

a Click **[item] available in** drop-down ..... `Alt`+`V`
arrow on left side of dialog box.

continued...

ORGANIZER (CONT.)

OR

Click **[item] available in** drop-down ..... `Alt`+`B`
arrow on right side of dialog box.

b Select desired document or template.... `↑↓`, `Enter`

OR

a Click `Close File` .... `Alt`+`F`
for open document/template on left side of dialog box.

OR

Click `Close File` .... `Alt`+`E`
for NORMAL.DOT on right side of dialog box.

b Click `Open File...` .... `Alt`+`F`
for **[item] available in** drop-down list box
on left side of dialog box.

OR

Click `Open File...` .... `Alt`+`E`
for **[item] available in** drop-down list box
on right side of dialog box.

c Follow procedures under **Open Document**,
page 15, to open desired file.

To copy items between documents and templates:

a Select item(s) to copy from either list box.

> 📖 *Select multiple consecutive items by
> holding down **Shift** and clicking each item.
> Select multiple, nonconsecutive items by
> holding down **Ctrl** and clicking each item.*

b Click `Copy ▶▶`  .... `Alt`+`C`

OR

Click `◀◀ Copy` 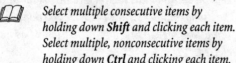 .... `Alt`+`C`

EDIT/FORMAT TEXT

To delete items from document or template:

a Select item(s) to delete from either list box.

b Click [Delete] .... Alt + D

c Click [Yes] .... Enter

OR

Click [Yes to All] .... Alt + A

To rename item in document or template:

a Select item to rename from either list box.

b Click [Rename...] .... Alt + R

c Type **New name** for item........................*new name*

d Click [OK] .... Enter

4 Click [Close] .... Esc

EDIT/FORMAT TEXT

AutoFormat

*This command does not format tables. To format tables automatically, use the **Table AutoFormat** command. (See page 170.)*

APPLY AUTOFORMAT

1   Select text to format.

2   Click **Format**, **AutoFormat** .... **Alt** + **O**, **A**

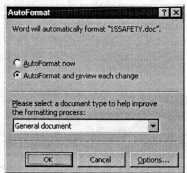

3   Select desired radio button option, if necessary.

4   Click   **OK**   .... **Enter**

*Word automatically formats the document with styles from the attached template. If you selected the **AutoFormat and review each change** radio button in step 3, the **AutoFormat** dialog box appears.*

5   Click desired **AutoFormat** command button(s) as necessary:

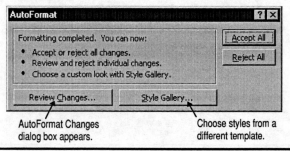

AutoFormat Changes dialog box appears.

Choose styles from a different template.

EDIT/FORMAT TEXT

REVIEW AUTOFORMAT CHANGES

*Appears when the **Review Changes** button is clicked in the above procedure, step 5.*

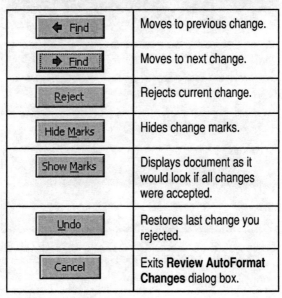

← Find	Moves to previous change.
→ Find	Moves to next change.
Reject	Rejects current change.
Hide Marks	Hides change marks.
Show Marks	Displays document as it would look if all changes were accepted.
Undo	Restores last change you rejected.
Cancel	Exits **Review AutoFormat Changes** dialog box.

EDIT/FORMAT TEXT

AUTOFORMAT OPTIONS

1   Click **Format**, **AutoFormat** .... `Alt`+`O`, `A`

2   Click `Options...` .... `O`

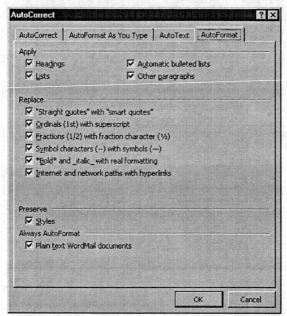

3   Click **AutoFormat** tab, if necessary .... `Ctrl`+`Tab`

4   Select document element(s) to **Apply**.

5   Select document element(s) to **Replace** automatically.

6   Click `OK` .... `Enter`

7   Click `OK`

EDIT/FORMAT TEXT

AUTOFORMAT AS YOU TYPE

1 Click **Fo**rmat, **A**utoFormat ....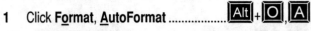

2 Click **Options...** ....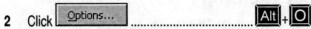

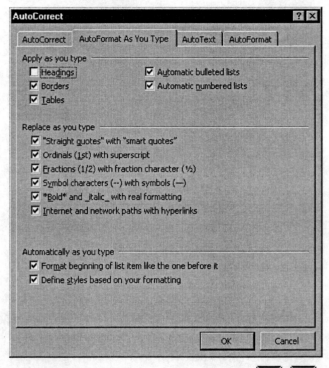

3 Click **AutoFormat As You Type** tab......... `Ctrl`+`Tab`
   if necessary.

4 Select document element(s) to AutoFormat as you type.

5 Click **OK** .... `Enter`

6 Click **OK**

EDIT/FORMAT TEXT

TABS

Set Tab Stop

SET TAB USING RULER

1 Select paragraph(s) to set tabs for.

2 Click **tab type** button ⌊L⌋ (default) on left end of horizontal ruler until desired tab type appears:

- ⌊L⌋ Left Tab
- ⌊I⌋ Bar Tab
- ⌊⊥⌋ Center Tab
- ▽ First Line Indent
- ⌊⌐⌋ Right Tab
- ⊔ Hanging Indent
- ⌊⊥⌋ Decimal Tab

📖 *For information on formatting paragraph indents, see page 106.*

3 Place arrow pointer on horizontal ruler where you wish to set tab stop.

4 Click mouse button.

To move tab:

Drag tab marker along horizontal ruler to desired tab-stop position.

SET TAB USING MENU

1 Select paragraph(s) to set tab stop(s) for.

2 Click **Format**, **Tabs** ....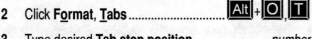

3 Type desired **Tab stop position** .... *number*

4 Select desired **Alignment** option:

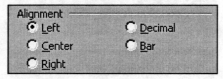

Alignment
- ⊙ **Left**
- ○ **Decimal**
- ○ **Center**
- ○ **Bar**
- ○ **Right**

5 Select **Leader** option, if desired:

124

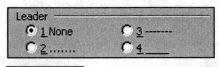

6 Click ‖ Set ‖ .... **Alt** + **S**

7 Repeat steps 3–6, as desired, to set additional
tab stops.

8 Click ‖ OK ‖ .... **Enter**

SET DEFAULT TAB STOPS

Tabs are set every .5" (half inch) by default.

*Default tab stops cannot be set for individual paragraphs, only
for an entire document or section. To set individual tab stops,
see the procedures above.*

1 Click **Format**, **Tabs** .... **Alt** + **O**, **T**

2 Click **Default tab stops** increment box ...... **Tab**, **↑↓**
and enter/select desired default tab-stop position.

3 Click ‖ OK ‖ .... **Enter**

CLEAR TAB STOP

CLEAR TAB USING RULER

1 Select paragraph(s) with tab stop(s) to clear.

2 Place arrow pointer on horizontal ruler, over tab stop
to clear.

3 Click and drag mouse down to pull tab marker off of
horizontal ruler.

4 Release mouse button.

5 Repeat steps 2–4 to clear additional tab stops.

EDIT/FORMAT TEXT

CLEAR TAB USING MENU

1 Select paragraph(s) with tab stop(s) to clear.

2 Click **Format**, **Tabs** .... `Alt`+`O`, `T`

3 Select tab stops to clear .... `↕`
from list box.

4 Click [Clear] .... `Alt`+`E`

*Moves tab stop(s) to the **Tab stops to be cleared** list. Clicking the OK button in step 6 removes the tabs. If you change your mind about any of the tabs in this list, cancel out of this dialog box.*

5 Repeat steps 3 and 4 to clear additional tab stops.
OR

Click [Clear All] .... `Alt`+`A`
to remove all tab stops.

6 Click [OK] .... `Enter`

GRAPHIC OBJECTS

*Each shape created using the drawing tools becomes an object which can be modified using the techniques described in **Modify Graphic Objects**, page 134.*

AutoShapes and Freeform Objects

*AutoShapes and freeform objects can also be accessed through the menu system; click **Insert**, **Picture**, **AutoShapes**, and the floating AutoShapes toolbar appears. The same options shown below in step 2, **Draw AutoShape**, are available in button form.*

DRAW AUTOSHAPE

1   Click **AutoShapes** on **Drawing** toolbar........

2   Click desired AutoShape category ....
    from the following menu options:

3   Select desired AutoShape ....
    to insert from pop-up palette.

The arrow pointer changes to a crosshair pointer: ╋

4   Position crosshair pointer where you wish to
    place AutoShape.

5   Drag until AutoShape object reaches desired
    dimensions.

continued...

Word Objects

To maintain object proportions while drawing:

Press **Shift** and drag mouse .... <kbd>Shift</kbd>+*drag*

To draw from object center:

Press **Ctrl** and drag mouse .... <kbd>Ctrl</kbd>+*drag*

> 📖 *Press **Ctrl+Shift** for both effects. Release mouse button before releasing **Ctrl** or **Shift** key.*

DRAW FREEFORM OBJECT

1 Click **AutoShapes** on **Drawing** toolbar ...... <kbd>Alt</kbd>+<kbd>U</kbd>

2 Click **Lines** .... <kbd>L</kbd>

3 Click **Freeform** 🔲 on pop-up palette.

   The arrow pointer changes to a crosshair pointer: +

4 Drag to draw freehand shape as desired.

   The crosshair pointer changes to a pencil: ✎

   To draw straight lines:

   a Click and release mouse button.

   b Move crosshair pointer to desired location and click.

5 Connect two ends of freeform shape.

   OR

   Double-click to exit freeform mode...................... <kbd>Esc</kbd>

Clip Art

INSERT CLIP ART

1 Click **Insert Clip Art** 🖼 on **Drawing** toolbar.

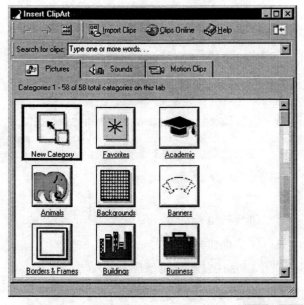

2 Click desired media tab .... `Ctrl`+`Tab`

3 Click desired category button .... `↕`, `Enter`

4 Click clip to insert............................ `↕`, `Enter`

A pop-up menu appears:

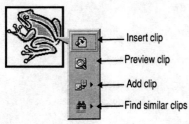

Insert clip
Preview clip
Add clip
Find similar clips

continued...

INSERT CLIP ART (CONT.)

5   Click **Insert clip**

To preview clip:

Click **Preview clip**

To add clip to Favorites or other category:

a   Click **Add clip**

b   Click **Category** drop-down arrow and select category.

c   Click ⬛ OK ⬛ .... Enter

To search for similar clips:

a   Click **Find similar clips**

b   Click desired hyperlink.

6   Click **Close** ❎ to exit Clip Gallery.

SEARCH FOR CLIPS

☞ FROM CLIP GALLERY

1   Click **Search for clips** text box.

2   Type keyword(s) and press **Enter**........ *keyword*,

DOWNLOAD CLIP ART FROM WEB

✦ FROM CLIP GALLERY

1 Click  .... **Alt**+**C**

2 Click OK .... **Enter**

You are connected to the following Web site: http://www.microsoft.com/clipgallerylive. From here, you may download many types of media from any of the available tabs.

3 Follow on-line directions.

> *When the **Download** dialog box appears, be sure to select the **Open** option, not the **Save to disk** option.*

4 Close **Insert ClipArt** dialog box to return to document.

IMPORT FILE INTO CLIP GALLERY

You can bring images, sounds, and motion clips into the Clip Gallery from other locations on your computer.

✦ FROM CLIP GALLERY

1 Click Import Clips .... **Alt**+**I**

   If the clip to insert is not a picture:

   Click **Files of type** drop-down arrow and select format.

2 Open drive and folder containing file to import.

3 Select desired clip import option.

   - **Copy into Clip Gallery**

   - **Move into Clip Gallery**

   - **Let Clip Gallery find this clip in its current folder or volume**

4 Double-click file to import.

continued...

IMPORT FILE INTO CLIP GALLERY (CONT.)

5 Type clip description....................................... *description*

6 Click **Categories** tab .... `Ctrl`+`Tab`

7 Select categories in which to place the clip.

To create a new category:

  a Click New Category... .... `Alt`+`N`

  b Type new category name.............................*name*

  c Click OK .... `Enter`

8 Click **Keywords** tab .... `Ctrl`+`Tab`

To add a new keyword:

  a Click New Keyword... .... `Alt`+`N`

  b Type new keyword .... *keyword*

  c Click OK .... `Enter`

To delete an existing keyword:

  a Select keyword to delete.

  b Click Remove Keyword .... `Alt`+`R`

9 Click OK .... `Enter`

Imported Pictures

INSERT PICTURE FROM FILE

1 Place cursor where you wish to insert picture.

2 Click **Insert Picture** 🖼 on **Picture** toolbar.

3 Locate and open picture to insert using the **Open Document** procedure. *(See page 15, for more information.)*

4 Click [Insert ▾] .... Enter

   OR

   a Click drop-down arrow next to [Insert ▾]

   b Select desired insert option .... ⬆⬇, Enter
      from the following:

      ■ **Insert** .... S

      ■ **Link to File** L
         Maintains link between picture and its source
         file. If you edit the source file, changes are
         updated in linked picture.

      ■ **Insert and Link** .... A

WORD OBJECTS

Modify Graphic Objects

DELETE OBJECT

1 Select object to delete.

2 Press **Delete** .... `Delete`

MOVE OBJECT

1 Select object(s) to move.

2 Drag the drag-and-drop-pointer ⟍ .... `↑↓ ←→`
     to new object location.

3 Click outside object(s) to deselect..................... `Enter`

SIZE OBJECT

Sizes an object manually by dragging sizing handles.

You can also size objects using the Format menu. In the Format menu, the command name changes to correspond to the selected Word object. The command icon is always the same

however: ✎

1 Select object to resize.

   The object is surrounded by eight sizing handles.

2 Position pointer over a sizing handle.

   The arrow pointer changes to a sizing pointer: ↔

3 Drag handle until object is desired size..

To maintain object proportions while sizing:

Press **Shift** while dragging .... Shift +*drag*
a corner sizing handle.

To size from object center:

Press **Ctrl** while dragging any handle .... Ctrl +*drag*

> 📖 *Press **Ctrl+Shift** for both effects. Release mouse*
> *button before releasing **Ctrl** or **Shift** key.*

CROP OBJECT

Crops object at 45 ° angles only. Do not confuse this feature
with the sizing feature. Cropping trims the object; sizing
changes the object's proportions.

You can also crop images using the menu system; click Format,
Picture, then click the Picture tab.

1 Select picture to crop.

2 Click **Crop** ⊹ on **Picture** toolbar.

The arrow pointer changes to a cropping tool:

3 Position cropping tool on corner to crop.

4 Click and hold down the mouse button as you drag
across picture to crop.

The cropping tool becomes directional: L

WORD OBJECTS

GROUP/UNGROUP OBJECTS

You may ungroup objects later to modify them individually.

1　Hold down the **Shift** key .... `Shift`*+click*
　and click each object to include in group.

　OR

　Select grouped object to ungroup.

2　Click **Dr̲aw** on **Drawing** toolbar .... `Alt`+`R`

3　Click **G̲roup** .... `G`

　OR

　Click **U̲ngroup** .... `U`

ALIGN OR DISTRIBUTE OBJECTS

1　Hold down the **Shift** key .... `Shift`*+click*
　and click each object to align or distribute.

2　Click **Dr̲aw** on **Drawing** toolbar .... `Alt`+`R`

3　Point to **Align or Distribute** .... `A`

4　Click desired alignment or distribution option:

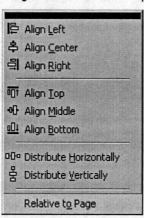

🖺 Align L̲eft
🕭 Align C̲enter
🖺 Align R̲ight
🖷 Align T̲op
🕩 Align M̲iddle
🖵 Align B̲ottom
ᴰᴰᵃ Distribute H̲orizontally
🖳 Distribute V̲ertically
Relative to̲ Page

To align object(s) relative to the page:

a   Click **Relative to Page** .... `Alt` + `O`

b   Repeat steps 2-4.

ROTATE/FLIP OBJECT

1   Select object(s) to rotate or flip.

2   Click **Draw** on **Drawing** toolbar .... `Alt` + `R`

3   Point to **Rotate or Flip** .... `P`

4   Click desired rotation or flip option:

ROTATE FREELY

1   Select object to rotate.

2   Click **Free Rotate** on **Drawing** toolbar.

The arrow pointer changes to:

*Four **rotate handles** appear at object's corners; they are small, bright green dots.*

3   Position pointer on any rotate handle.

The rotate pointer changes to:

4   Drag object to desired angle.

continued...

WORD OBJECTS

ROTATE FREELY (CONT.)

Object rotates from its center:

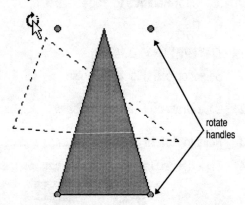

rotate handles

To rotate object from its corner:

Hold **Ctrl** while dragging.............................. `Ctrl` +*drag*

To rotate object at 15° intervals:

Hold **Shift** while dragging........................... `Shift` +*drag*

📖 *Press **Ctrl+Shift** for both effects. Release mouse button before releasing **Ctrl** or **Shift** key.*

ORDER OBJECTS

1 Select object to bring forward or backward.

2 Click **Draw** on **Drawing** toolbar.................. `Alt` + `R`

3 Point to **Order** .... `R`

4 Click desired layering option:

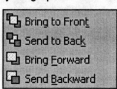

WORD OBJECTS

EDIT FREEFORM OBJECT

1 Select freeform object to edit.

2 Right-click selected object .... **Alt** + **R**

3 Click **Edit Points** .... **E**

4 Position arrow pointer on border to edit until arrow
   pointer changes to enhanced crosshair: ✛

5 Position crosshair over handle to move.

   Enhanced crosshair turns into: ✛

6 Click handle and drag to desired position.

7 Repeat step 6 as necessary to edit freeform object.

RESTORE PICTURE

1 Select picture to restore.

2 Click **Reset Picture** on **Picture** toolbar.

ADD SHADOW OR 3-D EFFECT

*To remove shadow or 3-D effect, select **No Shadow** or **No 3-D**
at top of pop-up palette in step 3.*

1 Select desired object.

2 Click **Shadow** or **3D Effect**
   on **Drawing** toolbar.

3 Click desired effect on pop-up palette ...... **↑↓ ←→** , **Enter**

WORD OBJECTS

EDIT OBJECT BORDER

CHANGE OBJECT BORDER COLOR

1 Select framed object.

2 Click **Format** .... `Alt`+`O`

The command name for the next step changes to correspond to the selected Word object. The command icon is the same in all instances, however.

3 Click 🖉 Auto**S**hape... or 🖉 Text B**o**x... `O`
   OR
   Click 🖉 P**i**cture... .... `I`

*The **Format [Object]** dialog box appears, where [Object] stands for the Word object chosen in steps 1 and 3.*

4 Click **Colors and Lines** tab, if necessary ... `Ctrl`+`Tab`

5 Click C**o**lor drop-down arrow .... `Alt`+`O`
   in **Line** section of dialog box.

6 Select desired border color .... `↕`, `Enter`
   from drop–down color palette.

To delete object border:

Click No Line .... `↑` `Enter`
at top of drop–down color palette.

7 Click OK

WORD OBJECTS

CHANGE OBJECT BORDER STYLE AND/OR WEIGHT

1 Open the **Format [Object]** dialog box. *(See Change Object Border Color, page 140.)*

2 Click **Colors and Lines** tab, if necessary ... `Ctrl`+`Tab`

3 Click **Style** drop-down arrow .... `Alt`+`S`
   in **Line** section of dialog box.

4 Select desired border style .... `⬆⬇`, `Enter`
   and point size from drop-down border palette.

5 Click **Weight** increment box .... `Alt`+`W`, `⬆⬇`
   and enter/select custom border width, if desired.

6 Click `OK`

SHADE OBJECT

1 Open the **Format [Object]** dialog box. *(See page 140.)*

2 Click **Colors and Lines** tab, if necessary ... `Ctrl`+`Tab`

3 Click **Color** drop-down arrow .... `Tab`
   in **Fill** section of dialog box.

4 Select desired fill color......................... `⬆⬇`, `Enter`
   in drop-down color palette.

   To delete object shading:

   Click `No Fill` .... `↑`, `Enter`

5 Select **Semitransparent** check box .... `Alt`+`T`

   Fills object with semitransparent shading, rather than opaque shading, if desired.

   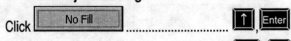 *This check box option is not available if object fill has been formatted with fill effects. (See Add Object Fill Effects, page 142.)*

6 Click `OK`

WORD OBJECTS

ADD OBJECT FILL EFFECTS

1 Open the **Format [Object]** dialog box. (*See steps 1-3,* ***Change Object Border Color****, page 140, for more information.*)

2 Click **Colors and Lines** tab, if necessary ...

3 Click **Color** drop-down arrow .... `Tab`, `↗↓`
in **Fill** section of dialog box.

4 Click **Fill Effects** .... `F`
at bottom of drop-down color palette.

   To add fill effects:

   a Click desired fill effects tab.

   b See **Fill Effects**, page 54.

   c Click `OK`

TEXT WRAPPING

1 Select object around which to wrap text.

2 Click **Format** menu .... `Alt`+`O`

   The command name for the next step changes to correspond to the selected Word object. The command icon is the same in all instances, however.

3 Click   `O`
   OR
   Click 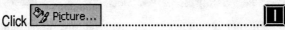 `I`

   *The **Format [Object]** dialog box appears, where [Object] stands for the Word object chosen in steps 1 and 3.*

4 Click **Layout** tab, if necessary................... `Ctrl`+`Tab`

5 Click desired **Wrapping style** option:

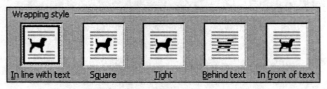

6 Select desired **Horizontal alignment** radio button option:

> 📖 *These options are unavailable if **In line with text** (default) is chosen in step 5.*

- **Left** .... Alt + L
  Places text to the right of the object;
  object is on left.

- **Center** .... Alt + C
  Wraps text around both sides of object.

- **Right** .... Alt + R
  Places text to the left of the object;
  object is on right.

- **Other** (default) .... Alt + O

7 Click ▐ OK ▐

WORD OBJECTS

TEXT BOXES

Positions or offsets text on a page, flows text from one part of a document to another, wraps text around a graphic, manipulates text as a graphic element. Standard character and paragraph formatting features are available within text boxes.

You can also insert graphic objects or tables in text boxes. See **Table Basics**, *page 150, and* **Graphic Objects**, *page 127, for more information. Please note that AutoShapes and WordArt must be grouped with their text boxes after insertion; otherwise, they behave like page elements and cannot be moved or manipulated together with their text boxes. See* **Group/Ungroup Objects**, *page 136.*

Create Text Box

Word automatically adds a border around a text box when you create it. To omit this border, click the **No Line** *button in step 6,* **Change Object Border Color**, *page 140.*

1 Click **Text Box** 📧 .... Alt + I , X
   on **Drawing** toolbar.

   Screen switches to Print Layout view. The arrow pointer changes to a crosshair: ⊹

2 Click where text box should begin and drag
   diagonally in desired direction to create text
   box of desired dimensions.

3 Release mouse button.

4 Type text in text box as desired.............................. *text*

ADD TEXT TO AUTOSHAPE

1 Right–click AutoShape to add text to.

2 Click **Add Text** X

3 Type text as desired .... *text*

4 Deselect AutoShape text box to exit text box.

WORD OBJECTS

Change Text Direction

✍ WITH TEXT BOX TOOLBAR DISPLAYED

1 Select text box with text to rotate.

2 Click **Change Text Direction** .... `Alt`+`O`, `X`
repeatedly until text has desired 90° rotation.

Set Text Box Margins

1 Select text box with margins to change.

2 Click **Format**, **Text Box** .... `Alt`+`O`, `O`

3 Click **Text Box** tab, if necessary .... `Ctrl`+`Tab`

4 Click increment box of each **Internal margin** to change
and enter/select desired margin space:

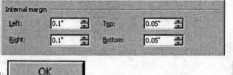

5 Click **OK** .... `Enter`

Link Text Boxes

✍ WITH TEXT BOX TOOLBAR DISPLAYED

1 Select first text box in linked chain.

2 Click **Create Text Box Link**

3 Click second text box in linked chain.

> *This text box should be empty so that text can flow
> from the first text box through the linked chain.*

*The arrow pointer changes to when positioned over
text box to link to chain.*

To remove text box link:

a Select first text box in linked chain.

b Click **Break Forward Link**

WORD OBJECTS

MOVE BETWEEN LINKED TEXT BOXES

✍ WITH TEXT BOX TOOLBAR DISPLAYED

1   Select desired text box.

2   Click **Next Text Box** 🔃

   OR

   Click **Previous Text Box** 🔃

WATERMARK

*See **Modify Graphic Objects**, page 134, for more information on formatting watermark objects.*

Standard character and paragraph formatting features are available within text boxes.

Add Watermark

1   Click **View**, **Header and Footer**............ `Alt` + `V`, `H`

2   Click **Show/Hide Document Text** 🔲 to select it.

3   Insert graphic object or text box as desired. *(See **Graphic Objects**, page 127, and **Text Boxes**, page 144, for more information.)*

4   Select Word object to convert to watermark.

5   Drag selected Word object to position it as desired.

6   Resize selected Word object by dragging a sizing handle, if desired.

7   Click **Format**... `Alt` + `O`

The command name for the next step changes to correspond to the selected Word object. The command icon is the same in all instances, however.

WORD OBJECTS

8   Click ⟨🖉 Auto**S**hape...⟩ or ⟨🖉 Text B**o**x...⟩ .... **O**

 OR

 Click ⟨🖉 **P**icture...⟩ .... **I**

 *The **Format [Object]** dialog box appears, where* [Object]
 stands for the Word object selected in steps 3 and 4.

9   Click **Layout** tab, if necessary..................... **Ctrl** + **Tab**

10 Click ⟨In line with text⟩ .... **Alt** + **I**
 as **Wrapping style** option, if necessary.

11 Click **C**olor drop-down arrow .... **Alt** + **C** , **↓** , **Enter**
 and click **Watermark**
 on drop–down list.

12 Click ⟨ OK ⟩

13 Click ⟨**C**lose⟩ .... **Alt** + **C**
 on **Header and Footer** toolbar.

WORD OBJECTS

WORDART

Insert WordArt

1 Select text on which to base WordArt.

2 Click **Insert WordArt** 4 .... `Alt`+`I`, `P`, `W`
 on **Drawing** toolbar.

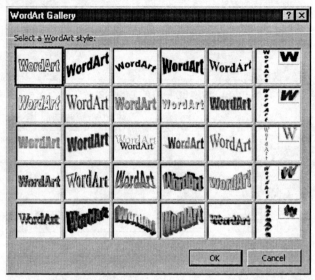

3 Double-click desired WordArt style .... ⬌, `Enter`

4 Edit/format selected text as desired.

5 Size and position WordArt object as desired.

6 Edit object as desired using WordArt toolbar.

> 📖 *Many WordArt styles include an adjustment*
> *handle ◇ (yellow diamond). Drag the*
> *adjustment handle to customize WordArt*
> *3-D effects. See **Size Object**, page 134.*

WordArt Toolbar

When you insert or select a WordArt object, the WordArt toolbar appears:

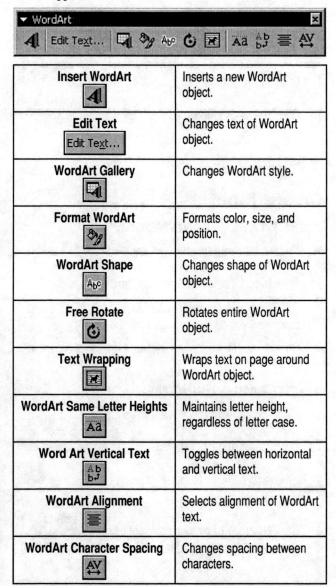

Insert WordArt	Inserts a new WordArt object.
Edit Text	Changes text of WordArt object.
WordArt Gallery	Changes WordArt style.
Format WordArt	Formats color, size, and position.
WordArt Shape	Changes shape of WordArt object.
Free Rotate	Rotates entire WordArt object.
Text Wrapping	Wraps text on page around WordArt object.
WordArt Same Letter Heights	Maintains letter height, regardless of letter case.
Word Art Vertical Text	Toggles between horizontal and vertical text.
WordArt Alignment	Selects alignment of WordArt text.
WordArt Character Spacing	Changes spacing between characters.

TABLES

TABLE BASICS

Display/Hide Gridlines

*Table gridlines that appear on screen do not print. If you want to print lines between table columns and rows, you need to add borders. (See **Borders and Shading**, page 59.)*

1   Click **Ta̲ble** .... `Alt`+`A`

2   Click **Show G̲ridlines** .... `G`
    OR

    Click **Hide G̲ridlines** .... `G`

Create Table

INSERT TABLE USING MOUSE

1   Place cursor where you want to insert table.

2   Click **Insert Table** ▦ on **Standard** toolbar.

3   Drag diagonally to select desired number of rows and columns from drop–down grid palette.

4   Click when table reaches desired number of columns and rows.

INSERT TABLE USING MENU

1   Place cursor where you want to insert table.

2   Click **Ta̲ble**, **I̲nsert**, **T̲able** .... `Alt`+`A`,`I`,`T`

3   Enter/select desired **Number of c̲olumns** .... `↕`
    (default is **5**).

4   Click **Number of r̲ows** increment box .... `Tab`,`↕`
    and enter/select desired number of rows (default is **10**).

5   Select desired **AutoFit behavior** radio button option:

- **AutoFit to contents** .... `Alt`+`F`

- **AutoFit to window** .... `Alt`+`D`

OR

a   Click **Fixed column width** .... `Alt`+`W`

b   Click increment box and enter/select .... 🔼
    desired column width (default is **Auto**).

6   Click `AutoFormat...` .... `Alt`+`A`
    if desired, to apply AutoFormat to new table.
    *(See **Table AutoFormat**, steps 3-6, page 170.)*

   To reset table default:
   Bases all new tables on changes made in this dialog box.

   Select **Set as default for new tables** .... `Alt`+`S`
   check box.

7   Click `OK` .... `Enter`

DRAW TABLE

1   Place cursor where you want to create table.

2   Click **Tables and Borders** 🔲 on **Standard** toolbar to
    display **Tables and Borders** toolbar, if necessary.

3   Verify that **Draw Table** ✏ on **Tables and Borders**
    toolbar is preselected.

    The arrow pointer changes to a pencil: ✏

4   Click and drag to draw table outline, columns, and rows.

    Pencil pointer changes to an enhanced pencil: ⌐✏

5   Deselect **Draw Table** ✏ to exit Draw Table mode.

TABLES

CONVERT TEXT TO TABLE

1   Select paragraphs to convert to a table.

2   Click **Ta**ble, Con**v**ert.............................. `Alt`+`A`, `V`

3   Click **Te**x**t to Table** .... `X`

4   Enter/select desired **Number of** **c**olumns .... `⬆⬇`

*By default, Word 2000 proposes a table size based on the text selected in step 1. Only the **Number of columns** can be adjusted in the dialog box.*

5   Select desired **AutoFit behavior** radio button option:

   ■   **Auto**F**it to contents** .... `Alt`+`F`

   ■   **AutoFit to win**d**ow**.............................. `Alt`+`D`

   OR

   a   Click **Fixed column** **w**idth.................. `Alt`+`W`

   b   Click increment box............................... `⬆⬇`
      and enter/select desired
      column width (default is **Auto**).

6   Click `AutoFormat...` .... `Alt`+`A`
   if desired, to apply AutoFormat to new
   table. *(See **Table AutoFormat**, steps 3-6, page 170.)*

7   Select code/character to convert to column markers in
   the **Separate text at** section of the dialog box:

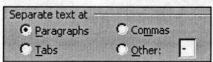

OR

a Select **Other** radio button...................... `Alt`+`O`
Converts each instance of specified
code/character to a column marker.

b Type character ....*character*
to convert to column marker
(default is - [hyphen]).

8 Click `OK` .... `Enter`

CONVERT TABLE TO TEXT

1 Select table to convert to paragraph text.

2 Click **Table**, **Convert**............................ `Alt`+`A`,`V`

3 Click **Table to Text**................................... `B`

4 Select code/character to **Separate text with**:

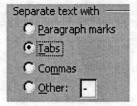

OR

a Select **Other** radio button...................... `Alt`+`O`
Converts each column marker
to the specified character.

b Type character ....*character*
to convert to column marker
(default is - [hyphen]).

5 Click `OK` .... `Enter`

TABLES

Insert Cells, Rows, and Columns

INSERT CELL(S)

1 Select a cell or group of cells.

> 📖 *The number of new cells added will equal the number of cells selected.*

2 Click **Insert Cells** 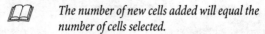 .... **Alt**+**A**, **I**, **E**
on **Standard** toolbar.

3 Select desired placement for new cell(s) relative to selected cell(s):

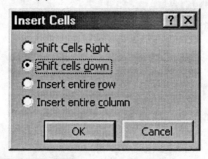

4 Click **OK** .... **Enter**

INSERT ROW(S)

To insert new row at end of table:

Place cursor in last cell of last row in table........... **Tab**
and press **Tab**.

1 Select a row or group of rows.

> 📖 *The number of new rows added will equal the number of rows selected.*

2 Click **Insert Rows** on **Standard** toolbar.

New rows are inserted above selected rows by default. You may need to adjust row height. (See page 161 for more information.)

154

OR

a Click **Table**, **Insert** ....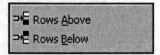

b Select desired placement for new row(s) from menu options:

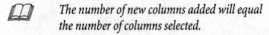

INSERT COLUMN(S)

1 Select a column or group of columns.

> *The number of new columns added will equal the number of columns selected.*

2 Click **Insert Columns** on **Standard** toolbar.

New columns are inserted to the left of the selected columns by default. You may need to adjust column width. (See page 158 for more information.)

OR

a Click **Table**, **Insert** ....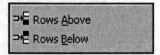

b Select desired placement for new column(s) from menu options:

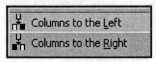

TABLES

Delete Cells, Rows, and Columns

DELETE CELL(S)

1   Select cell or group of cells to delete.

2   Click **T**a**b**le, **D**elete, C**e**lls .... **Alt** + **A**, **D**, **E**

3   Select desired placement for remaining cells:

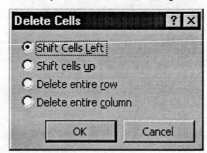

4   Click **OK** .... **Enter**

DELETE ROW(S)/COLUMN(S)

1   Select row(s) or column(s) to delete.

2   Click **T**a**b**le, **D**elete, **R**ows or **C**olumns ...... **Ctrl** + **X**

OR

Click **E**dit, Cu**t** .... **Shift** + **Delete**

Table Placement

FLOATING TABLE

⚘ FROM WEB LAYOUT VIEW OR PRINT LAYOUT VIEW

1 Scroll to upper-left corner of page with table to move.

2 Position I-beam pointer $\underline{\text{I}}$ anywhere inside table to move.

¤	Nov.¤	Dec.¤	Jan.¤	¤
Nuts¤	354¤	231¤	132¤	¤
Bolts¤	859¤	348¤	448¤	¤
Screws¤	383¤	394¤	505¤	¤

table move handle

table resize handle

3 Position arrow pointer over table move handle ⊞ until move arrow appears:

To resize table:

a Position arrow pointer over table resize handle ☐ until sizing arrow appears: ⤢

b Click and drag to size table as desired.

4 Click and drag to place table as desired.

TEXT WRAPPING (TABLE)

1 Create and place table as desired using procedure above.
   OR

   Draw table, as desired .... **Ctrl**+*drag*

   using **Draw Table** 🖉 on **Tables and Borders** toolbar while holding down the **Ctrl** key. *(See page 151 for more information.)*

2 Click **Table, Table Properties** .... **Alt**+**A**,**R**

3 Click **Table** tab, if necessary .... **Alt**+**T**

4 Click Around .... **Alt**+**A**

5 Click OK .... **Enter**

TABLES

Adjust Column Width

AUTOFIT

1 Position arrow pointer over a gridline until it turns into a column sizing handle:

2 Right-click mouse button.

3 Click **AutoFit** .... A

4 Click desired AutoFit menu option:

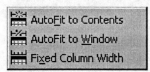

OR

1 Select column(s) to adjust.

2 Click **Table**, **AutoFit** .... Alt + A, A

3 Complete step 4, above.

DISTRIBUTE EVENLY

1 Select row(s) or column(s) to adjust.

2 Click **Distribute Rows Evenly** ⊞ on **Tables and Borders** toolbar.

OR

Click **Distribute Columns Evenly** ⊞

ADJUST COLUMN WIDTH USING MOUSE

You can also adjust column widths by dragging the column gridlines. When adjusting columns using gridlines, you do not need to select the column first. When the arrow pointer is positioned over a gridline, it turns into a column sizing arrow.

1 Select column to adjust.

2 Position arrow pointer on column marker ▦ on horizontal ruler.

   A ScreenTip appears next to the sizing pointer:

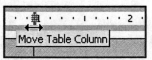

3 Click and hold down mouse button as you drag column marker ▦ to desired position.

   Whether you drag column gridlines or column markers along the ruler, the following procedures apply:

   - Dragging the mouse by itself causes only selected columns or cells to resize.

   - Holding down **Shift** while dragging adjusts overall table width to accommodate column change.

   - Holding down **Shift**+**Ctrl** while dragging proportionally adjusts all columns and cells to right of selected columns or cells.

   - Holding **Ctrl** adjusts selected columns or cells immediately to the right of selected columns or cells.

TABLES

ADJUST COLUMN WIDTH USING MENU

1 Select column(s) to adjust.

2 Double–click column marker ▦ .... **Alt**+**A**, **R**
  on horizontal ruler.

3 Click **Colu̲mn** tab, if necessary .... **Alt**+**U**

4 Apply column **Size** settings, as necessary:

    a Select **Preferred w̲idth** check box .... **Alt**+**W**

    b Enter/select desired column-width measurement
       in increment box.

    c Adjust column-width unit of measure, if necessary,
       in **Measure in** drop-down list box (default
       is **Inches**).

To change width of other columns:

Click [◀◀ P̲revious Column] .... **Alt**+**P**

OR

Click [N̲ext Column ▶▶] .... **Alt**+**N**

5 Click [OK] .... **Enter**

Adjust Row Height

ADJUST ROW HEIGHT USING MOUSE

✍ IN PRINT LAYOUT VIEW

1 Select row to adjust.

2 Position arrow pointer on vertical ruler row marker.

A ScreenTip appears next to the sizing pointer:

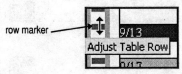

3 Click and hold down mouse button as you drag row marker to desired position.

4 Release mouse button.

ADJUST ROW HEIGHT USING MENU

1 Select row(s) to adjust.

2 Double–click column marker ▦ .... `Alt`+`A`, `R`
on horizontal ruler.

3 Click **Row** tab, if necessary .... `Alt`+`R`

4 Apply row **Size** settings, as necessary:

   a Select **Specify height** check box .... `Alt`+`S`

   b Enter/select desired row-height measurement
      in increment box.

   c Indicate new row measurement's parameters
      in **Row height is** drop-down list box
      (e.g., **At least**, **Exactly**).

continued...

TABLES

ADJUST ROW HEIGHT USING MENU (CONT.)

5 Select/deselect any other desired **Options:**

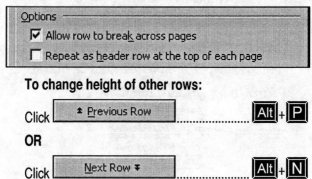

To change height of other rows:

Click **⬆ Previous Row** .... **Alt** + **P**

OR

Click **Next Row ⬇** .... **Alt** + **N**

6 Click **OK** .... **Enter**

Merge and Split

MERGE CELLS

When cells are merged together, the contents of each are converted to paragraphs within the combined cell.

1 Select cells to merge.

2 Click **Merge Cells** .... `Alt`+`A`,`M`
on **Tables and Borders** toolbar.

SPLIT CELLS

1 Select cell or group of cells to split.

2 Click **Split Cells** .... `Alt`+`A`,`P`
on **Tables and Borders** toolbar.

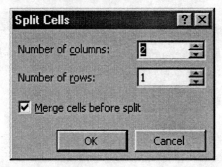

3 Adjust increment box settings, if necessary.

4 Click [OK] .... `Enter`

SPLIT TABLE

1 Place cursor in row to establish as first row of new table.

2 Click **Table**, **Split Table** .... `Shift`+`Ctrl`+`Enter`

To remove a split, delete the paragraph mark between the two tables. You may also need to reformat one or both tables. (See page 170.)

TABLES

TABLE TEXT

Insert Tabs in Cells

1 Place cursor where you wish to insert a tab.

2 Press **Ctrl+Tab**.. `Ctrl` + `Tab`

Insert Table Headings

Sets Word to recognize selected information as headings, which it will then automatically repeat on each page of a table spanning more than one page.

If a hard page break is inserted into the table, however, table headings are not repeated.

1 Select row to designate as table headings.

2 Click **Table**, **Heading Rows Repeat** ... `Alt` + `A`, `H`

   Heading information is automatically copied and pasted into the top row of each page that the table spans.

Sort Text

1 Select text to sort.

2 Click **Sort Ascending** ⏏ on **Tables and Borders** toolbar.

   OR

   Click **Sort Descending** ⏏

ADVANCED SORTING OPTIONS

1 Select text to sort.

2 Click T**a**ble, **S**ort .... `Alt`+`A`,`S`

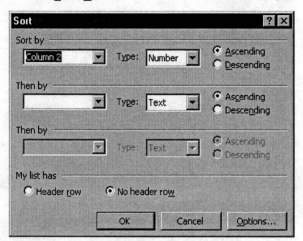

3 Select first–tier sort options:

   a Select first item to **Sort by** (e.g., **Column** [number], **Paragraphs**, **Field** [number], or **Name**).

   b Click **Type** drop-down arrow and select text type to sort.

   c Select desired sort direction.

4 Select second–tier sort options:

   📖 *The options shown below may not be available, depending on choices made in step 3.*

   a Click **Then by** drop-down arrow and select second item to sort by.

   b Click **Type** drop-down arrow and select text type to sort (e.g., **Date**, **Number**, **Text**).

   c Select desired sort direction.

continued...

ADVANCED SORTING OPTIONS (CONT.)

5 Select third–tier sort options:

📖 *The options shown below may not be available,*
depending on choices made in steps 3 and 4.

a Click second **Then by** drop-down arrow and select third item to sort by.

b Click **Type** drop-down arrow and select text type to sort.

c Select desired sort direction.

6 Select desired **My list has** option, if necessary:

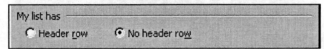

To access additional sort options:

a Click Options... .... **Alt**+**O**

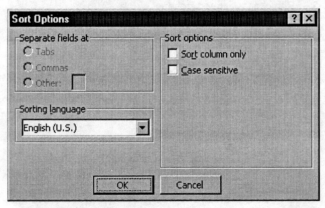

b Select desired sort options.

c Click OK .... **Enter**

7 Click OK .... **Enter**

TABLE FORMULA BASICS

*In Word tables, formulas are inserted as fields. These fields are able to perform mathematical calculations using cell references. A **cell reference** refers to a cell's column letter and row number (e.g., A1, A2, B1, B2, etc.). Formulas consist of the following:*

equal sign	=
calculation function	=SUM
open parenthesis	=SUM(
cell range to calculate	=SUM(C1:C5
close parenthesis	=SUM(C1:C5)
COMPLETE FORMULA	**=SUM(C1:C5)**

Cells are referenced as follows:

- **Column calculation** — *Cell ranges are referred to as ABOVE or BELOW the cursor. For example, =SUM(ABOVE) adds all cells above the cursor.*

- **Row calculation** — *Cell ranges are referred to as LEFT or RIGHT of the cursor. For example, =SUM(LEFT) adds all cells to the left of the cursor.*

- **Contiguous range** — *Type starting and ending cells, separated by a colon. For example, =SUM(C1:C5) adds all cells between A1 and C5.*

- **Noncontiguous range** — *Type cell references, separated by commas. For example, =SUM(A1,B1) adds cells A1 and B1.*

*The default calculation for a table is addition (SUM function). If you select the **Formula** command when your cursor is in a table, Word evaluates the location of the cursor and attempts to calculate the most logical cell range using the SUM function.*

*(See **Fields**, page 83, for information on updating and working with fields.)*

TABLES

AutoSum

Adds the values above or to the left of the cursor, inserting the result of a column or row calculation in the selected cell.

This total does not update automatically if new values are added to the table. You must repeat this procedure to update your total.

1 Place cursor in cell to contain total.

2 Click **AutoSum** $\boxed{\Sigma}$ on **Tables and Borders** toolbar.

Insert Formula

1 Place cursor in cell to contain formula.

2 Click **Table, Formula** .... **Alt** + **A**, **O**

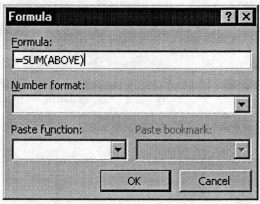

3 Type **Formula** and cell range as desired (including equal sign, function name, parentheses, and cell range). *(See page 167, Table Formula Basics, for more information.)*

OR

a Click **Paste function** drop-down arrow and select desired function:

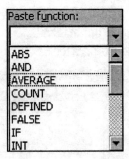

Selected function is inserted after equal sign in **Formula** *text box. The cursor appears inside the first (or only) set of parentheses, next to the function name.*

b Type cell range inside each set .... *cell range* of parentheses.

4 Click **Number format** drop-down arrow and select desired number format from drop-down list box.

> *If the numbers being calculated include a number format (e.g., percentage), the formula result automatically appears in that format.*

5 Click OK .... Enter

Results of formula appear in selected cell.

TABLES

TABLE FORMATS

Table AutoFormat

1   Select table to AutoFormat.

2   Click **Table AutoFormat** 📑 .... **Alt** + **A**, **F**
    on **Tables and Borders** toolbar.

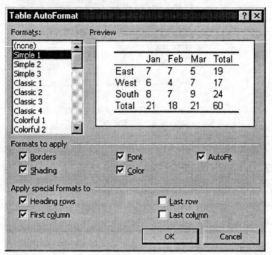

3   Select desired AutoFormat from **Formats** list box.

4   Adjust AutoFormat's basic design elements, if desired,
    by deselecting any of the **Formats to apply** options:

5   Adjust AutoFormat's advanced design elements, if
    desired, by selecting or deselecting any of the following
    Apply special formats to options:

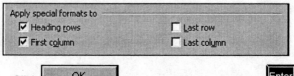

6   Click [OK] .... **Enter**

BOOKMARKS

1 Select text to bookmark.

2 Click **Insert**, **Book̲mark** .... Shift + Ctrl + F5

3 Type **B̲ookmark name** ....*name*

  OR

  Select name of bookmark to redefine ....
  from list box.

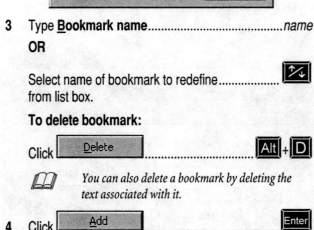

  To delete bookmark:

  Click [**D̲elete**] .... Alt + D

  You can also delete a bookmark by deleting the text associated with it.

4 Click [**A̲dd**] .... Enter

Go to Bookmark

You can also jump to a bookmark using the Go To command.
(See page 25.)

 If bookmarks do not display, select the
Bookmarks check box in the View tab of the
Options dialog box (Tools, Options). See
Screen Display Options, page 50.

1   Click **Insert**, Boo**k**mark .... `Shift`+`Ctrl`+`F5`

2   Select bookmark to go to.. `↑↓`
    in **Bookmark name** list box.

3   Click `Go To` .... `Alt`+`G`

4   Click `Close` .... `Esc`

CAPTIONS

*(See **Fields**, page 83, for information on updating and working*
with fields.)

1   Select object to add caption to.

2   Click **Insert**, **C**aption .... `Alt`+`I`,`C`

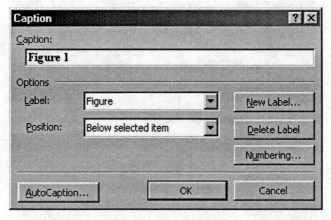

ADVANCED CAPTION OPTIONS

- **New Label** button   Click to create new label name.

- **Numbering** button   Click to change number format. *See **Customize Numbered List**, page 68.*

- **AutoCaption** button   Click to add captions each time you insert selected item.

3   Type desired **Caption** text .... , *text* (defaults to the label name shown in the **Label** drop-down list box, followed by a number).

EXAMPLE:

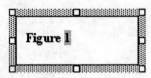

To change label name:

a   Click **Label** drop-down arrow ....

b   Select appropriate label name .... (e.g., **Equation**, **Figure**, or **Table**).

OR

To delete a label:

i   Select **Label** to delete ....

ii   Click ....

   *Captions are positioned below the selected object by default. If you wish to place them above the object, make this change in the **Position** drop-down list box.*

4   Click ....

REFERENCES

CROSS-REFERENCES

*Cross-references in Word, created with REF fields, refer to footnotes, endnotes, bookmarks, captions, or paragraphs created using heading styles. (See **Fields**, page 83, for more information on updating and working with fields.)*

1   Place cursor where you want to insert cross-reference.

Word suggests you type the text that introduces the cross-reference (e.g., For more information, see . . .).

2   Click **Insert**, **Cross-reference** .... `Alt`+`I`, `R`

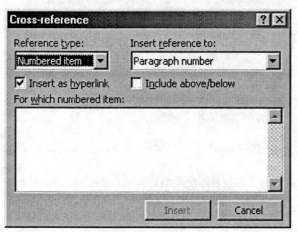

    *The choices in the **Cross-reference** dialog box vary depending on the available reference items in the active document.*

3   Select item to reference in **Reference type** drop-down list box.

4   Click **Insert reference to** drop-down arrow and select type of information to display in cross-reference.

For example, you could select a chapter heading or page number. The cross-reference might read: See also Getting Started or page xx. Word inserts the heading or page number and automatically updates them after any changes.

5   Verify that the **Insert as hyperlink** .... <kbd>Alt</kbd>+<kbd>H</kbd>
    check box is selected (default).

> 📖 *This option allows the on-line reader to move*
> *directly from a cross-reference to the*
> *referenced item in the same,*
> *master document.*

6   Select object to refer to in **For which [selected object]**
    list box.

7   Click [Insert] .... <kbd>Alt</kbd>+<kbd>I</kbd>

8   Click [Close] .... <kbd>Esc</kbd>

FOOTNOTES/ENDNOTES

Insert Footnote or Endnote

INSERT FOOTNOTE/ENDNOTE USING SHORTCUTS

1   Place cursor where you want to insert footnote/endnote.

2   Press **Ctrl+Alt+F** .... <kbd>Ctrl</kbd>+<kbd>Alt</kbd>+<kbd>F</kbd>
    to insert footnote.

    OR

    Press **Ctrl+Alt+E** .... <kbd>Ctrl</kbd>+<kbd>Alt</kbd>+<kbd>E</kbd>
    to insert endnote.

> 📖 *If last footnote or endnote inserted in document*
> *used **AutoNumber** format, the next consecutive*
> ***AutoNumber** footnote or endnote is inserted. If*
> *last footnote or endnote inserted in document*
> *used a **Custom mark**, the Footnote and Endnote*
> *dialog box appears. See illustration on next page*
> *for more information.*

3   Type footnote or endnote text as desired .... *text*

4   Click [Close] .... <kbd>Shift</kbd>+<kbd>Alt</kbd>+<kbd>C</kbd>

REFERENCES

INSERT FOOTNOTE/ENDNOTE USING MENU

1   Place cursor where you want to insert footnote/endnote.

2   Click **Insert**, **Foot***n***ote** .... **Alt** + **I** , **N**

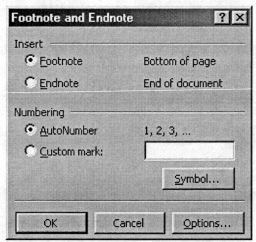

ADVANCED FOOTNOTE AND ENDNOTE OPTIONS

- **Symbol** button   Click to insert special character.
  *See **Insert Symbol**, page 80.*

- **Options** button   Click to adjust note placement,
  format, sequence, etc.

3   Select desired note type to **Insert**.

4   Select desired **Numbering** style, if necessary.

5   Click   OK   .... **Enter**

6   Type footnote or endnote text as desired .... *text*

7   Click   Close   .... **Shift** + **Alt** + **C**

View Footnote or Endnote

By default, footnotes and endnotes are visible when the document is viewed in Print Preview or Print Layout View.

Further, positioning the arrow pointer over a reference mark displays a ScreenTip containing the linked note text. The arrow pointer turns into a note I-beam: [3] 🔲 *Double-click the reference mark to enter the note pane for editing. See Screen Display Options, page 50, for more information.*

You can also move between footnotes or endnotes using the Go To command. (See page 25.)

Convert Footnotes or Endnotes

1 Click **Insert**, **Foot<u>n</u>ote**.......................... `Alt`+`I`,`N`

2 Click `Options...` .... `Alt`+`O`

3 Click named tab of notes to convert:

   - **All <u>F</u>ootnotes** .... `Alt`+`F`

   - **All <u>E</u>ndnotes** .... `Alt`+`E`

4 Click `Convert...` .... `Alt`+`T`

5 Select desired conversion option:

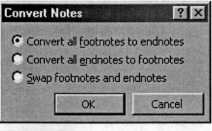

6 Click `OK` .... `Enter`

7 Click `OK` twice .... `Enter`, `Enter`

REFERENCES

INDEX AND TABLES

*Indexes and tables in Word 2000 are created using fields. When you have edited a document so that page numbers or text included in a table have (has) changed, you must update the table. To do so, click anywhere in table to select it, then press the F9 key. (See **Fields**, page 83, for information on working with fields.)*

Index

Click **Show/Hide ¶** ⊤ , if desired, on **Standard** toolbar to display or hide index entries.

MARK INDEX ENTRY

*To refer to multiple pages in an entry, mark all text to refer to with a bookmark. (See **Bookmarks**, page 171.)*

1 Select text to use as index entry.

   OR

   Place cursor where you want to insert index entry.

2 Press **Shift+Alt+X**.............................. `Shift`+`Alt`+`X`

   OR

   a Click **Insert**, **Index and Tables** .... `Alt`+`I`, `D`

   b Click **Index** tab, if necessary................. `Alt`+`X`

   c Click Mark Entry... .... `Alt`+`K`

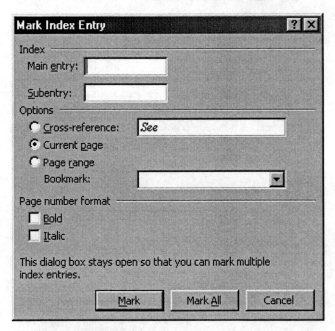

3 Type or edit index entry text .... *text*
in **Main entry** text box.

*Text selected in step 1 appears in the **Main entry** text box automatically.*

4 Click **Subentry** text box, if desired .... , *text*
and type subentry text.

> *To include a third–level entry, type the subentry text followed by a colon and the third–level text.*

continued...

MARK INDEX ENTRY (CONT.)

5 Select desired reference **Options**:

- **Cross–reference**........................ **Alt**+**C**, *text*
  Lists cross–reference text (rather than a page number) in the index entry. Type cross–reference text as desired, formatting cross–reference text using shortcut keys. *(See **Character Formatting**, page 73.)*

- **Current page** (default)...................... **Alt**+**P**
  Lists current page number in index entry.

- **Page range**.. **Alt**+**R**
  Lists a page range in the index entry.

  *To use **Page range** option, you must first mark the page range to refer to with a bookmark. Then, select the bookmark name from the **Bookmark** drop–down list box.*

6 Select desired **Page number format** check box option(s), as desired:

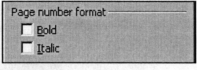

7 Click [Mark] .... [Enter]

 OR

 Click [Mark All] .... **Alt**+**A**

 Marks first occurrence in each paragraph that exactly matches letter cases in selected entry.

To mark multiple index entries:

*The **Mark Index Entry** dialog box stays open in Word 2000. Navigate through the document and select text to mark as index entry. Then, click **Main entry** text box in the **Mark Index Entry** dialog box, verify index entry text and repeat step 7, above.*

8   Click [Close] .... Esc
    when indexing is complete.

COMPILE INDEX

1   Place cursor where you want to insert index, typing any heading text necessary (e.g., *Index*, *List of References*, etc.).

2   Click **Insert**, In**d**ex and Tables .... Alt + I, D

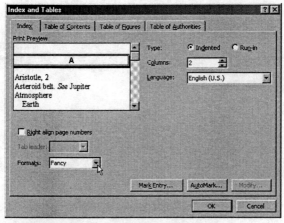

ADVANCED INDEX AND TABLES OPTIONS

- **Right align page numbers** check box

  Select to align page numbers with right margin. Select desired **Tab leader** if you select this check box. *See **Set Tab Stop**, page 124.*

- **Modify** button

  Click to create custom index format. *See **Apply Style**, page 110.*

continued...

COMPILE INDEX (CONT.)

3 Click **Index** tab, if necessary ....

> 📖 *Note the **Print Preview** scroll list box in the top-left corner of the dialog box.*

4 Select desired index **Type**, if necessary:

5 Change number of **Columns**, if necessary.

6 Click **Formats** drop-down arrow and select desired index format:

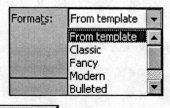

7 Click  .... Enter

Table of Contents

MARK TABLE OF CONTENTS ENTRY

*Word 2000 compiles a table of contents based on heading styles applied to document text. (See **Styles**, page 110, for more information.) To mark table of contents entries manually, complete the procedure below.*

*You can also use styles that include outline-level formats. (See **Customize Multilevel List**, page 71, for more information.)*

1   Select text to use as table entry.

   OR

   Place cursor where you want to insert table entry.

2   Press **Shift+Alt+O**.............................. Shift + Alt + O

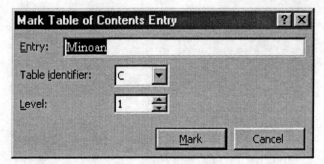

3   Edit or type table **Entry** text...*text*

*Text selected in step 1 appears in the **Entry** text box automatically.*

   If you have more than one contents list:

   Click **Table identifier** drop-down arrow, then select group letter of contents list to add entry to.

4   Click **Level** increment box and enter/select desired entry level, if necessary.

5   Click [Mark] .... Enter

REFERENCES

COMPILE TABLE OF CONTENTS

By default, Word 2000 compiles a table of contents from heading styles, although you can also use other styles and table entry fields. Further, Word right aligns page numbers with a dot leader by default.

1 Place cursor where you want to insert table of contents, typing any heading text necessary (e.g., *Contents, Table of Contents*).

2 Click **Insert**, **Index and Tables** .... `Alt`+`I`, `D`

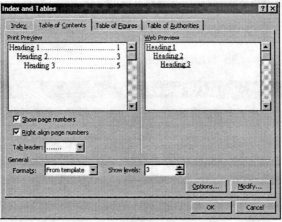

ADVANCED TABLE OF CONTENTS OPTIONS

■ **Show** page numbers **Right align page numbers**	Deselect these check box options if desired.
■ **Tab leader** drop-down arrow	Change tab leader style if desired. *See **Set Tab Stop**, page 124.*
■ **Options** button	Click to compile table of contents using custom heading styles or field entries.
■ **Modify** button	Click to create custom table-of-contents format. *See **Apply Style**, page 110.*

REFERENCES

3 Click **Table of <u>C</u>ontents** tab .... `Alt`+`C`
   if necessary.

4 Click **Forma<u>t</u>s** drop-down arrow and select desired
   table of contents format.

5 Click **Show <u>l</u>evels** increment box and enter/select
   number of entry levels to list in table of contents,
   if necessary.

6 Click ` OK ` .... `Enter`

REFERENCES

Table of Figures

CREATE TABLE OF FIGURES

*Word 2000 compiles a table of figures based on labeled captions. (See **Captions**, page 172, for more information.) If you have labeled your figures manually, you can apply a custom style to identify those labels as captions—upon which you can then build a table of figures.*

You can also use styles or table entry fields to build a table of figures.

1   Place cursor where you want to insert table of figures, typing any heading text necessary (e.g., *Illustrations, Table of Figures, Plates*).

2   Click **I**nsert, In**d**ex and Tables............ `Alt`+`I`,`D`

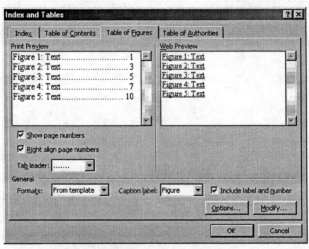

ADVANCED TABLE OF FIGURES OPTIONS

▪	**Show** page numbers **Right** align page numbers	Deselect these check box options if desired.
▪	**Tab** leader drop-down arrow	Change tab leader style if desired. *See **Set Tab Stop**, page 124.*

- **Options** button   Click to compile table of figures using custom heading styles or field entries.

- **Modify** button   Click to create custom table-of-figures format. *See **Apply Style**, page 110.*

3 Click **Table of Figures** tab .... `Alt`+`F` if necessary.

4 Click **Formats** drop-down arrow and select desired table of figures format.

5 Verify **Caption label** setting; change if necessary.

6 Select **Include label and number** .... `Alt`+`N` check box, if necessary, to include captions in the table of figures.

7 Click `OK` .... `Enter`

REFERENCES

Table of Authorities

Tables of authorities are created using long citations and short citations. Long citations in a legal document are used only once and contain the entire text of the citation. All further references to the same source are short citations containing a summary of the corresponding long citation.

MARK CITATION

1 Select information to use as a long citation.

   OR

   Place cursor where you want to insert a citation entry.

2 Press **Shift+Alt+I** .... `Shift`+`Alt`+`I`

   OR

   a Click **Insert**, **Index and Tables** .... `Alt`+`I`, `D`

   b Click **Table of Authorities** tab.............. `Alt`+`A`
       if necessary.

   c Click `Mark Citation...` .... `Alt`+`K`

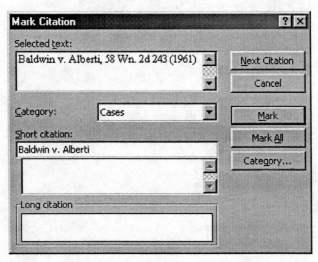

ADVANCED MARK CITATION OPTIONS

- **Next Citation** button — Click to mark multiple citations. Locates next citation in document.

- **Category** drop-down arrow — Click to create custom category.

*Text selected in step 1 appears in the **Selected text** and **Short citation** text boxes automatically.*

 *You can format citation entries in **Mark Citation** dialog box using shortcut keys. (See **Character Formatting**, page 73.)*

3 Click **Selected text** text box and create or edit long citation text to search for when compiling table of authorities.

4 Click **Category** drop-down arrow and select desired citation category.

5 Create or edit **Short citation** text to search for when compiling table of authorities.

6 Click [Mark] .... [Enter]

OR

Click [Mark All] .... [Alt]+[A]

Marks all occurrences of short and long citations.

7 Click [Close] .... [Esc]

COMPILE TABLE OF AUTHORITIES

1 Mark document citations using procedure above.

2 Place cursor where you want to insert table of authorities, typing any heading text necessary (e.g., *Table of Authorities, Cases*).

3 Click **Insert**, **Index and Tables** .... [Alt]+[I],[D]

continued...

COMPILE TABLE OF AUTHORITIES (CONT.)

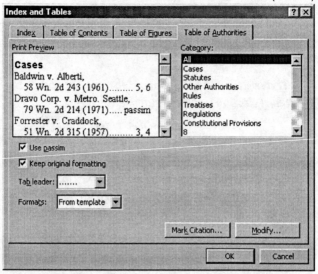

ADVANCED TABLE OF AUTHORITIES OPTIONS

- **Use passim**
  Keep original formatting

  Deselect these check box options if desired.

- **Tab leader**
  drop-down arrow

  Change tab leader style if desired. *See Set Tab Stop, page 124.*

- **Modify** button

  Click to create custom table of authorities format. *See Apply Style, page 110.*

4 Click **Table of Authorities** tab .... **Alt**+**A**
   if necessary.

5 Click **Category** list box and select category
   to compile citations for.

6 Click **Formats** drop-down arrow and select desired
   table of authorities format.

7 Click [OK] .... **Enter**

PROOFING TOOLS

AUTOCORRECT

1 Place cursor anywhere in document.

OR

Select text to AutoCorrect.

2 Click **Tools**, **AutoCorrect** .... Alt + T, A

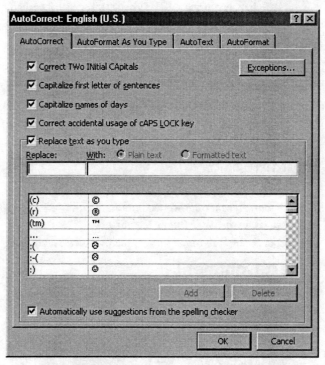

AUTOCORRECT OPTIONS

- **Exceptions** button

  Stores exceptions with mixed letter cases.

- **Replace text as you type** check box

  Click to add new AutoCorrect entry. Then, enter the text you wish to replace; indicate what you wish to replace text with.

continued…

Proofing Tools

- **Replace** text box — Select entry to edit from list box, then click **Replace** button after entering correction in **With** text box.

- **Delete** button — Select entry to delete from list box, then click **Delete** button.

- **Automatically use suggestions from the spelling checker** check box — Deselect this option if desired.

3 Click **AutoCorrect** tab, if necessary .... `Ctrl`+`Tab`

4 Select/deselect desired AutoCorrect options.

5 Click `OK` .... `Enter`

COMMENTS

Reviewers' comments appear in a document as hidden text; they are marked with color-coded initials. See also **Discussions**, *in the Word Online section, page 232, to use Word 2000's new Web-dimension for the Comments feature.*

Insert Comment

By default, Word uses the user name and initials entered in the User Information tab of the **Options** *dialog box (Tools, Options).*

1 Place cursor where you want to insert comment.

2 Click **Insert Comment** 📝 .... `Ctrl`+`Alt`+`M`
   on **Reviewing** toolbar.

   OR

   Click **Insert**, **Comment** .... `Alt`+`I`, `M`

   To adjust comments pane, see **Split Window**, *page 3.*

3 Type comment text as desired .... *text*

4 Click `Close` .... `Shift`+`Alt`+`C`

PROOFING TOOLS

Display Comment

You can jump to a comment using the Go To command. (See page 25 for more information.)

Rest pointer on top of yellow-shaded text.

Reviewer's name and comment appears:

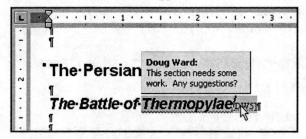

 *If comments do not display, select the **ScreenTips** check box in the View tab of the **Options** dialog box (Tools, Options). See **Screen Display Options**, page 50.*

Edit Comment

1   Select comment mark of comment to edit.

    OR

    a   Double-click comment mark of comment to edit.

    b   Skip to step 3.

2   Click **Edit Comment** .... `Alt`+`V`, `C`
    on **Reviewing** toolbar.

    OR

    Click **Delete Comment** on **Reviewing** toolbar.

Click to select reviewer
comments to display.

continued...

3   Make desired changes in comments pane.

4   Click `Close` .... `Shift` + `Alt` + `C`

Review Comments

Comments can be printed with the document or by themselves.
*(See **Print Document**, page 22.)*

Click **Previous Comment** 🔲 on **Reviewing** toolbar.

OR

Click **Next Comment** 🔲.

PROOFING TOOLS

FIND AND REPLACE

Allows you to find and replace text, graphics, fields, and special items in a document. You can also find and replace fonts, styles, and various other formatting attributes.

Find Text

*You can search for formatting elements without typing any text in the **Find what** text box in step 4. Simply include formatting to find in the **Find and Replace** dialog box using formatting shortcut keys in the **Find what** text box. Otherwise, refer to **Search Options**, page 196, for more information.*

1   Place cursor where you want to begin search.

2   Click **Edit**, **Find** .... `Ctrl`+`F`

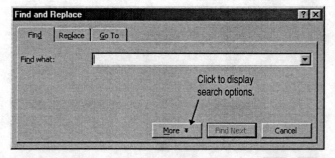

Click to display search options.

3   Click **Find** tab, if necessary .... `Alt`+`D`

4   Type text to search for in **Find what** text box...........*text*
    OR

    Click **Find what** .... `F4`, `↕`, `Enter`
    drop–down arrow and select
    from list of last four search entries.

5   Click **Find Next** .... `Enter`

6   Click **Cancel** .... `Esc`
    to close **Find and Replace** dialog box.

PROOFING TOOLS

Find Again

Click **Next Find/GoTo** ⬇ .... `Ctrl` + `Page Down`

on vertical scroll bar to move down through the document.

OR

Click **Previous Find/GoTo** ⬆ .... `Ctrl` + `Page Up`

to move up through the document.

Search Options

Using this procedure you can also locate: font style, paragraph formatting, tab types, language criteria, frames, styles, and highlighting.

1   Complete steps 1-4, **Find Text**, page 195.

2   Click [More ⬇] .... `Alt` + `M`

    to display more search options.

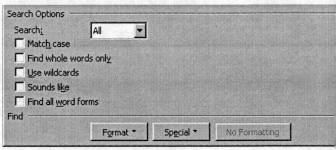

3   Select desired **Search Options**.

    To set search direction:

    Click **Search:** drop-down arrow to select desired
    search direction.

    To find formatting or formatted text:

    a Click [Format ▾] and select formatting to find
        from pop-up menu.

    b Select desired formatting options to find.

PROOFING TOOLS

To clear all formatting:

Click `No Formatting` .... **Alt** + **T**

To search for special character:

Click `Special ▼` and select special character to find.

4 Click `Find Next` .... **Enter**

Replace Text

1 Place cursor where you want to begin search.

2 Click **Edit**, **Replace** .... **Ctrl** + **H**

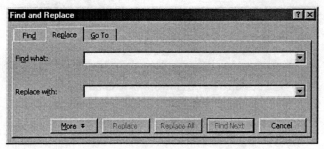

3 Type text to search for in **Find what** text box........... *text*

OR

Click **Find what** drop–down arrow and select from list of last four search entries.

4 Click **Replace with** text box and type replacement text to insert.

OR

Click **Replace with** drop–down arrow and select from list of last four replacement entries.

continued...

REPLACE TEXT (CONT.)

To clear all formatting:

Click [No Formatting] .... `Alt` + `T`

*For more search options, see **Search Options**, page 196, if necessary. To apply these options to the replacement text, make sure the cursor is in the **Replace with** text box while you select/deselect desired search options.*

5   Click desired Find and Replace button(s), as necessary:

- [Replace] .... `Alt` + `R`

  Replaces occurrence with new text/format.

- [Replace All] .... `Alt` + `A`

  Replaces all occurrences.

- [Find Next] .... `Enter`

  Locates next occurrence of text/format.
  This option does not replace text or format.

6   Click [Cancel] .... `Esc`

to close **Find and Replace** dialog box.

PROOFING TOOLS

HIGHLIGHTER PEN

To remove highlighting, select highlighted text and click the
Highlight *button.*

1   Click **Highlight** 🖍️▾ on **Formatting** or **Reviewing**
    toolbar.

    The arrow pointer becomes a highlighter I-beam: 🖍️

2   Select text to highlight.

    To change highlighting color:

    Click drop–down arrow next to **Highlight** 🖍️▾ and
    select desired highlight color.

3   Repeat step 2 to highlight additional text, if desired.

4   Deselect **Highlight** 🖍️▾ .... Esc
    to turn off highlighting.

PROOFING TOOLS

HYPHENATION

Automatic hyphenation is turned off by default. You can turn it on using this procedure. You can also hyphenate your document manually by completing the manual hyphenation option shown at the bottom of this page.

1 Click **Tools**, **Language** .... **Alt** + **T**, **L**

2 Click **Hyphenation** .... **H**

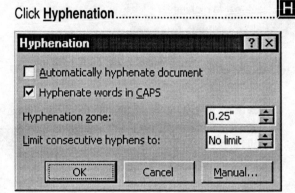

3 Select desired hyphenation check box option(s).

4 Click **Hyphenation zone** .... **Alt** + **Z**, ⬆⬇
increment box and enter/select desired
distance from right margin in which to
hyphenate words (default is **0.25"**).

5 Click **Limit consecutive** .... **Alt** + **L**, ⬆⬇
hyphens to increment box and
enter/select maximum number of
lines to end in hyphens (default is **No limit**).

To hyphenate a document manually:

Allows you to approve or reject each hyphenation in the document.

a   Click `Manual...` .... `Alt`+`M`

b   Click mouse to change position to **Hyphenate at**.

c   Click `Yes` .... `Alt`+`Y`
   Hyphenates word at position shown
   in the text box.

   OR

   Click `No` .... `Alt`+`N`
   Rejects current hyphenation and moves
   to next word to hyphenate.

d   Click `OK` .... `Enter`
   once manual hyphenation is complete.

6   Click `OK` .... `Enter`

PROOFING TOOLS

PROTECT DOCUMENT

*You can protect Word documents so that reviewers can make comments, but not revisions; or so that reviewers can make marked revisions only; or so that users can fill in form fields, but cannot otherwise alter the file. (See **Comments**, page 192. Also see **Save Document**, page 19, for information on assigning a password to prevent a document from being opened and/or modified.)*

1 Click **Tools**, **Protect Document** .... **Alt** + **T**, **P**

2 Select desired **Protect document for** radio button option:

3 Type **Password**, if desired .... *password*
   OR
   Skip to step 4.

4 Click **OK** .... **Enter**

5 **Reenter password to open** .... *password*

6 Click **OK** to confirm .... **Enter**

PROOFING TOOLS

Unprotect Document

1 Click **Tools, Unprotect Document**...... Alt + T , P

2 Type **Password**, if necessary .... *password*

3 Click OK .... Enter

SPELLING AND GRAMMAR

*Grammar is checked by default in Word 2000. To check spelling only, deselect the **Check grammar** check box in the Spelling and Grammar dialog box. (See also page 4.)*

1 Place cursor where you want to begin spelling and grammar check.

OR

Select text to check.

2 Click **Spelling and Grammar** [icon] F7
   on **Standard** toolbar.

OR

Click **Tools, Spelling and Grammar**... Alt + T , S

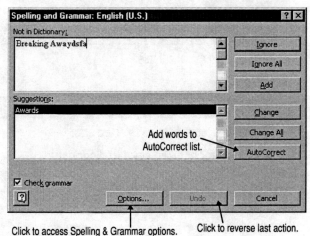

Click to access Spelling & Grammar options.   Click to reverse last action.

continued...

PROOFING TOOLS

SPELLING AND GRAMMAR (CONT.)

*The Spelling and Grammar dialog box appears with a spelling or grammar error displayed in the top window. The title of this window varies, depending on the error. You can edit the errors displayed, and suggested solutions are frequently available in the **Suggestions** list box.*

To replace error with suggestion:

a Click **Suggestions** list box and select desired suggestion.

b Click [Change] .... **Alt**+**C**

to replace selected occurrence of error with suggested alternative.

OR

Click [Change All] .... **Alt**+**L**

to replace all occurrences of selected error with selected suggestion.

To leave error unaltered and continue checking:

Click [Ignore] .... **Alt**+**I**

OR

Click [Ignore Rule] .... **Alt**+**G**

to ignore grammatical rule.

OR

Click [Ignore All] .... **Alt**+**G**

to skip all occurrences of selected error.

To add unrecognized word to dictionary:

Click [Add] .... **Alt**+**A**

3 Click [Close] .... **Esc**

to close **Spelling and Grammar** dialog box after changes are complete.

PROOFING TOOLS

Spelling and Grammar Options

Customizes Word's Spelling operation. Also activates custom or supplemental dictionaries to check words that Spelling doesn't recognize, such as technical terms or foreign words.

1   Click **Tools**, **Options**............................ Alt + T , O

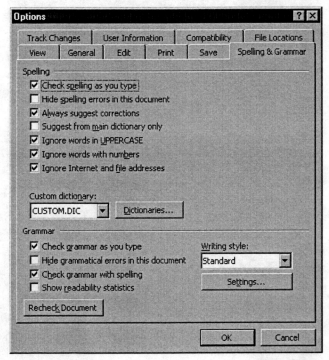

2   Click **Spelling & Grammar** tab .... Ctrl + Tab
    if necessary.

3   Verify/change **Spelling** and/or **Grammar** options
    as desired.

4   Click [OK] .... Enter

PROOFING TOOLS

THESAURUS

1   Select word for which you want to find a synonym, antonym, or related word.

2   Click **Tools**, **Language**, **Thesaurus** .... `Shift` + `F7`

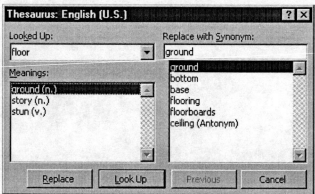

3   Make desired selection(s) in **Meanings/Alphabetical List** and/or **Replace with Synonym** list box(es).

4   Click Replace .... `Alt` + `R`

PROOFING TOOLS

TRACK CHANGES

*Marks revisions to document so you can track changes and differentiate between several reviewers' changes. You can accept or reject any marked change. The way revision marks are displayed is set in the Track Changes tab of the **Options** dialog box (Tools, Options). See **Screen Display Options**, page 50, for more information.*

Turn Track Changes On

*When Track Changes is turned on, the **TRK** indicator in the status bar is bold. To verify/specify Highlight Changes features to activate, use the menu steps below.*

Double–click **Track Changes** TRK .... Ctrl + Shift + E
on status bar.

OR

1   Click **Tools, Track Changes** .... Alt + T , T

2   Click **Highlight Changes** .... H

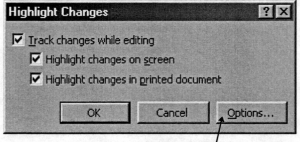

Click to access Track Changes options.

3   Click [OK] .... Enter

PROOFING TOOLS

Turn Track Changes Off

Double–click **Track Changes** `TRK` .... `Ctrl`+`Shift`+`E`
on status bar.

OR

1   Complete steps 1 and 2, **Turn Track Changes On**,
    above.

2   Deselect **Highlight changes on screen** and **Highlight
    changes in printed document** check boxes.

3   Click `OK` .... `Enter`

Review Changes

ACCEPT/REJECT CHANGES USING MOUSE

*You can also use the shortcut menu feature to accept/reject
changes. Simply right-click on a change and select **Accept
Change** or **Reject Change**. (See also **Shortcut Menus** in the
Basics section, page 4.)*

      ✍ WITH REVIEWING TOOLBAR DISPLAYED

1   Place cursor where you want to start review.

2   Locate change(s):

    ▪ **Previous Change** 🔖

    ▪ **Next Change** 🔖

3   Accept or reject change(s) as desired:

    ▪ **Accept Change** 🔖

    ▪ **Reject Change** 🔖

4   Repeat steps 2 and 3 as necessary.

PROOFING TOOLS

ACCEPT/REJECT CHANGES USING MENU

1   Double–click **Track Changes** `TRK` .. `Ctrl`+`Shift`+`E`
    on status bar.

2   Place cursor where you want to start review.

3   Click **Tools**, **Track Changes** .... `Alt`+`T`,`T`

4   Click **Accept or Reject Changes** .... `A`

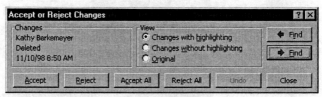

To accept/reject individual changes:

a   Click `← Find` or `⇨ Find` .... `I` or `F`
    to select change to review.

b   Click `Accept` or `Reject` .... `A` or `R`

To accept/reject all changes:

a   Click `Accept All` or `Reject All` .... `C` or `J`

b   Click `Yes` .... `Enter`
    when confirmation dialog box appears.

5   Click `Close` .... `Esc`

PROOFING TOOLS

Compare Versions

Compares two versions of a document, inserting revision marks where a revised document differs from the original.

1   Open revised version of document.

2   Click **T**ools, **T**rack Changes .... `Alt`+`T`,`T`

3   Click **C**ompare Documents .... `C`

4   Click **Files of type** drop-down arrow and select type of file to compare with the current document, if necessary.

5   Open file to compare with current document. *(See **Open Document**, page 15.)*

    Word compares documents and marks changes in current one.

6   Accept or reject marked revisions in current document. *(See **Review Changes**, page 208.)*

Merge Revised Documents

Merges revisions/comments from the revised document into the original document.

1   Open document in which to display merged revision marks/comments from all documents.

2   Click **T**ools, Merge **D**ocuments .... `Alt`+`T`,`D`

3   Click **Files of type** drop-down arrow and select type of file to merge with the current document, if necessary.

4   Open file to merge with current document. *(See **Open Document**, page 15.)*

5   Repeat steps 2-4 for each additional document to merge.

PROOFING TOOLS

WORD COUNT

1 Click **Tools**, **Word Count**.................... Alt + T , W

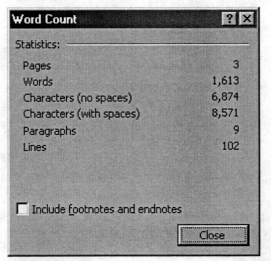

2 Click ⬚ Close .... Esc

MAIL OPTIONS

ENVELOPES AND LABELS

*To print envelopes using a file containing names and addresses, see **Mail Merge**, page 214.*

Create Envelope

1   Click **Tools**, **Envelopes and Labels** ... `Alt`+`T`, `E`

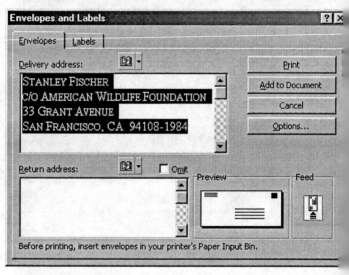

*If Word 2000 detects an address in the open document, that address appears in the **Delivery address** text box.*

2   Click **Envelopes** tab, if necessary .... `Alt`+`E`

3   Edit or type **Delivery address**.

4   Click **Return address** text box and type return address or verify default address.

> *The default return address is the **Mailing address** entered in the User Information tab of the **Options** dialog box (Tools, Options). If you make changes to the return address, a prompt will appear after step 5 asking if the new return address is to be saved as default.*

To omit return address from envelope:

Select **Omit** check box .... Alt + M

5 Click [Print] .... Alt + P

OR

Click [Add to Document] .... Alt + A

Adds envelope to document. Envelope
prints with document when you complete
the **Print Document** procedure, page 22.

> *When you add an envelope to a document,
> Word inserts a section break before or after the
> document text.*

Create Mailing Label

1 Click **Tools**, **Envelopes and Labels** ... Alt + T , E

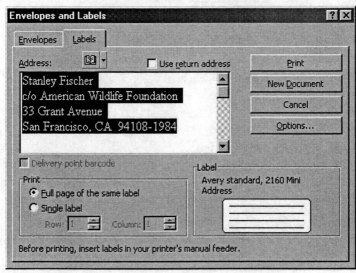

*If Word 2000 detects an address in the open document,
that address appears in the **Address** text box.*

continued…

MAIL OPTIONS

CREATE MAILING LABEL (CONT.)

2   Click **Labels** tab, if necessary .... **Alt** + **L**

3   Edit or type **Address**.

    OR

    Select **Use return address** check box .... **Alt** + **R**
    to create return-address labels instead.

> 📖 *The default return address is the **Mailing**
> **address** entered in the User Information tab of
> the **Options** dialog box (Tools, Options).*

4   Select **Full page of the same label** radio button, if
    necessary, to print selected address on every label
    of sheet.

    OR

    a   Select **Single label** radio button to print address on
        a single label of sheet.

    b   Click **Row** increment box and enter/select row
        number containing label to print address on.

    c   Click **Column** increment box and enter/select
        column number containing label to print address on.

5   Click 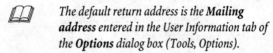 .... **Alt** + **P**

MAIL MERGE

*A mail merge combines the contents of a main document and a
data source. A **main document** contains information that
does not change, such as the body of a form letter. A **data**
source contains information, known as records, that varies
with each merged document (e.g., names, addresses).*

*Creating a mail merge involves several steps: creating the main
document, creating the data source, inserting merge fields into
the main document, and then merging the two completed
documents. The **Mail Merge Helper** is a Word feature
designed to assist in this process.*

The following procedures describe how to set up a basic mail merge. (See your Word documentation, or refer to online Help, for information on advanced options and techniques.)

Set Up Mail-Merge Main Document

This command can also be used to restore a mail-merge main document back to a normal Word document.

1 Open document to use as main document,
   or create new document to use. *(See **Open Document**, page 15, and **Create New Document**, page 13.)*

2 Click **Mail Merge Helper** .... `Alt`+`T`,`R`
   on **Mail Merge** toolbar.

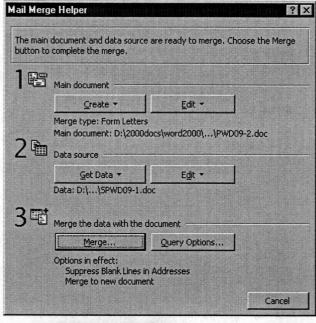

3 Click `Create ▾` .... `Enter`

4 Select type of merge document to set up:

continued...

SET UP MAIL-MERGE MAIN DOCUMENT (CONT.)

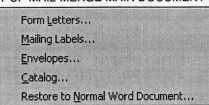

Form Letters...

Mailing Labels...

Envelopes...

Catalog...

Restore to Normal Word Document...

> 📖 The **Restore to Normal Word Document**
> option is only available if the active document
> is already a mail-merge main document.

*A prompt appears, asking if you want to use the active
window or if you would like to create a new document to
use as the mail-merge main document.*

5 Click ⬚ Active Window ⬚ .... `Enter`
  to use displayed document as main document.
  OR

  Click ⬚ New Main Document ⬚ .... `Alt`+`N`
  to open a blank document.

6 Click ⬚ Edit ▼ ⬚ .... `Alt`+`E`, `Enter`

  The mail-merge main document reopens.

7 Edit or type generic main-document text.

> 📖 *This text remains the same for all versions.*

8 Complete the **Attach Data Source** procedure,
  page 219, to insert personalized name and address
  information.

Mail Merge Toolbar

*After creating a mail-merge main document, the **Mail Merge** toolbar appears:*

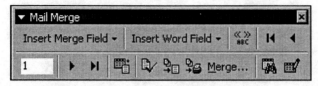

BUTTON	DESCRIPTION
Insert Merge Field ▾	Inserts merge field into document at cursor location.
Insert Word Field ▾	Inserts Word field into document at cursor location.
View Merged Data «» ABC	Toggles between displaying merge fields and data-source records.
First Record ⏮	Displays first record in attached data source.
Previous Record ◀	Displays the previous record in the attached data source.
Go to Record 1	Selects specific record to display from attached data source.
Next Record ▶	Displays next record in attached data source.
Last Record ⏭	Displays last record in attached data source.
Mail Merge Helper	Displays **Mail Merge Helper** dialog box.

continued...

MAIL OPTIONS

MAIL MERGE TOOLBAR (CONT.)

Check for Errors	Checks the mail merge for errors.
Merge to New Document	Merges main document and data source to new document.
Merge to Printer	Merges main document and data source to printer.
Start Mail Merge Merge...	Displays **Merge** dialog box, which is used for selecting specific records to merge, query options, and other choices when merging main document and data source.
Find Record	Searches for specific record in attached data source.
Edit Data Source	Displays **Data Form** dialog box, which is used for managing records in data source.

MAIL OPTIONS

Attach Data Source

*Creates a new data source or opens an existing one. This command also allows you to specify a separate header-row file for the data source. A **header row** is the top row in a data-source table that contains merge fields. **Merge fields** identify the various types of information contained in each column of the data source.*

CREATE DATA SOURCE

1   Complete the **Set Up Mail-Merge Main Document** procedure, page 215.

2   Click **Mail Merge Helper** 📋 .... Alt + T , R
    on **Mail Merge** toolbar.

3   Click [Get Data ▼] .... Enter , C
    and click **Create Data Source**.

> *This option is only available if the active file is set up as mail-merge main document.*
>
> *A mail-merge data source contains columns of data labeled by field names, which appear in the header row. Commonly used field names are listed in **Field names in header row** list box. You can add, remove, or rearrange these default names to create a custom header row.*
>
> *The header row must contain the same number of field names as there are field columns in the data source.*

continued...

Mail Options

CREATE DATA SOURCE (CONT.)

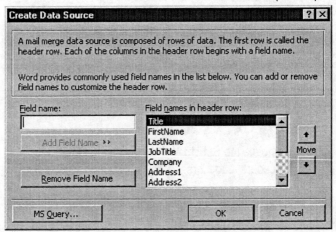

To add a custom field name to header-row list:

a Click **Field name** text box .. `Alt`+`F`, *field name*
and type new field name.

b Click `Add Field Name ▶▶` .... `Alt`+`A`

To remove a field name from header-row list:

a Click **Field names in header row** list box
and select field name to remove.

b Click `Remove Field Name` ...... `Alt`+`R`

To reorder field names in header-row list:

a Click **Field names in header row** list box
and select field name to move.

b Click **Move Up** `↑` or **Move Down** `↓`

4 Click `OK` .... `Enter`
once header-row list is complete.

5 Save new data source. *(See **Save Document**, page 19.)*

A prompt appears, telling you that there is no data in your new data source. You are asked whether you want to edit the data source by adding data records to it, or if you would like to edit the main document by adding merge fields to it.

6 Click Edit Data Source .... Enter

*The **Data Form** dialog box appears. The field names selected in the **Create Data Source** dialog box appear in the left-hand column of the dialog box, with blank text boxes across from them:*

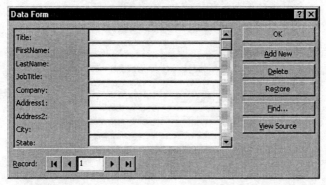

7 Add new record(s) to data source:

   a Press **Tab** or **Shift+Tab** to move between fields.

   b Type desired information into field name text boxes, as necessary.

   c Click Add New .... Alt + A

   d Repeat steps a–c to include additional records.

continued...

MAIL OPTIONS

To move between records:

Click one of the following navigation buttons:

- **First Record**   - **Next Record** ▶

- **Previous Record** ◀   - **Last Record** ▶│

OR

Click **Record** text box.........................*number*, Enter
and type desired record number.

8   Click desired command buttons to edit, find, or view
    data-source file records:

▪ **Delete**	Removes record from data source.
▪ **Restore**	Restores record to its original contents.
▪ **Find...**	Searches data source for information.
▪ **View Source**	Allows you to view data-source file in table form.

📖   *Viewing the data-source file in table form allows
     you to edit data records using the Database toolbar.*

9   Click **OK** ....Enter

*Word reopens the main document. When you close the
main document, you will be prompted to save changes to
the data-source document as well.*

OPEN EXISTING DATA SOURCE

1   Complete the **Set Up Mail-Merge Main Document** procedure, page 215.

2   Click **Mail Merge Helper** 🖼️ .... `Alt`+`T`, `R` on **Mail Merge** toolbar.

3   Click `Get Data ▼` .... `Enter`, `O` and click **Open Data Source**.

> 📖   *This option is only available if the active file is set up as mail-merge main document.*

4   Click **Files of type** drop-down arrow, if necessary, to display other source file types (e.g., Microsoft Access files, Excel files, etc.).

5   Open file containing desired data. *(See **Open Document**, page 15.)*

Insert Merge Fields into Main Document

INSERT MERGE FIELD USING MOUSE

1   Place cursor in mail-merge main document where you want to insert merge field.

2   Click `Insert Merge Field ▼` on **Mail Merge** toolbar.

3   Select desired merge field .... ⬚ from available merge fields on drop-down list:

continued...

INSERT MERGE FIELD USING MOUSE (CONT.)

4 Repeat steps 1–3 to insert additional merge fields.

INSERT MERGE FIELD USING MENU

1 Place cursor in mail-merge main document where you want to insert merge field.

2 Press **Shift+Alt+F** .... Shift + Alt + F

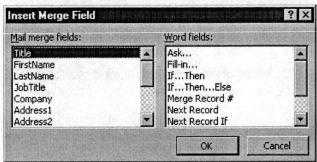

3 Select from available **Mail merge fields** to insert.

4 Click OK .... Enter

5 Navigate through mail-merge main document to insert additional merge fields, including spacing and punctuation as desired.

6 Repeat steps 1–5 to insert additional merge fields.

Preview Merged Documents

Lets you view the merged documents before printing. Use this feature to see if the merge fields are in the correct positions in the main document.

1 Open the mail-merge main document.

2 Click **View Merged Data** on **Mail Merge** toolbar.

3 Deselect **View Merged Data** to return to mail-merge main document.

Merge Documents

1   Open the mail-merge main document.

2   Click **Merge to New Document** 🔳... Alt + Shift + N
    to create a new document containing
    all merged form documents.

    OR

    a   Click **Merge to Printer** 🔳...... Alt + Shift + M
        to send all merged form documents
        directly to the printer.

    💣   *Be sure to preview merged documents*
            before sending them to the printer or
            you may end up with errors that could
            have been corrected before printing. See
            Preview Merged Documents, *above.*

    b   Complete steps 2-4, **Print Document**, page 22.

ADVANCED DOCUMENT MERGE

*From the **Merge** dialog box, users can have Word 2000 check*
for and report errors in the Merge process. Users can also set up
a merge query in which data records can be filtered and sorted
as desired. For more information on these options, please
consult online Help or your Word 2000 documentation.

1   Open the mail-merge main document.

2   Click **Start Mail Merge** Merge... .... Alt + M

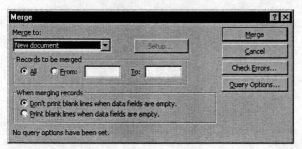

continued...

MAIL OPTIONS

ADVANCED DOCUMENT MERGE (CONT.)

3 Click document type to **Merge to**:

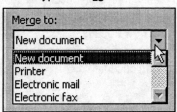

  *If you merge the document to **Electronic mail**
or **Electronic fax**, click the **Setup** button to
access the **Merge To Setup** dialog box.*

4 Select **Records to be merged**, if necessary.

5 Select desired **When merging records**
radio button option.

6 Click  .... Enter

WEB TOOLBAR

Allows you to access and navigate the Internet from within a Word 2000 document in Web Layout view (shown on the following page) or via Microsoft Internet Explorer.

1 Display Web toolbar.
2 Click button on Web toolbar to access Internet as desired:

Start Page	Alt + G, S	Opens the default home page.
Search the Web	Alt + G, W	Allows you to pick a search engine and begin an Internet search.
Favorites ▾	n/a	Select from Web sites designated as your favorites.
Go ▾	Alt + G	Provides Web-navigation options.
Address bar drop-down list	n/a	Select from previously visited Web sites or file locations on your hard drive.

continued...

WEB TOOLBAR (CONT.)

Show Only Web Toolbar (selected)

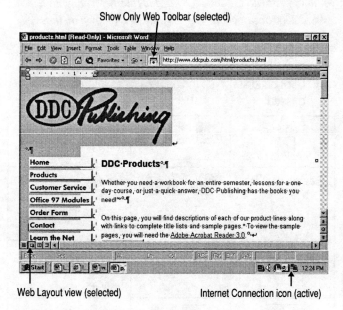

Web Layout view (selected)　　　　　Internet Connection icon (active)

3 Sign in as necessary using your ISP's (or online service's) instructions.

OFFICE MAIL

Sends the open file in an e-mail message as an attachment.

1 Click **Send to Mail Recipient**  on **Reviewing** toolbar.

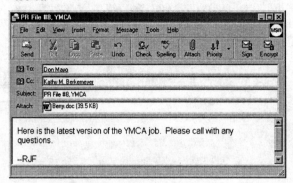

2 Enter/select document recipients.

3 Verify **Subject** line; edit as necessary.

4 Type e-mail message as desired.................... *message*

5 Click Send .... **Alt** + **S**

WORD ONLINE

ONLINE MEETING

Shows a document over a network, enabling colleagues in various locations to collaborate in real time.

Online collaborations require a network setup using standard networking protocol and valid user names for computers using a network or the Internet.

Schedule Online Meeting

1 Click **Tools**, **Online Collaboration**...... Alt + T , N

2 Click **Schedule Meeting** .... S

> *If **Microsoft NetMeeting** dialog box appears, enter your personal information and select desired Directory.*
>
> *Complete **Outlook 2000 Startup**, if necessary.*

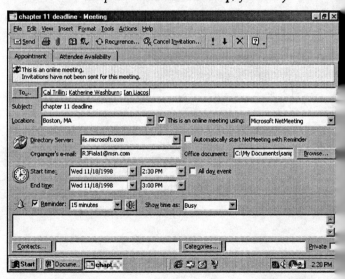

3 Click **Appointment** tab, if necessary .... Ctrl + Tab

4 Complete invitation form, as desired.

To access Outlook address book:

Click `To...` .... `Alt`+`.`

To view attendees' schedules:

Click **Attendee Availability** tab .... `Ctrl`+`Tab`

5 Click `Send` .... `Ctrl`+`Enter`
on **Meeting Standard** toolbar.

Begin Online Meeting

1 Complete **Schedule Online Meeting**, above.

2 Click **Call Participant** on **Online Meeting** toolbar.

3 Enter/select individuals to invite to online meeting.

4 Click `Call` .... `Enter`

WORD ONLINE

DISCUSSIONS

Discussions in Word 2000 allow you and your colleagues to conduct "discussions" in documents, organizing and threading multiple replies beneath the original comment. This allows authors to keep track of reviewers' comments without comparing multiple paper drafts.

1   Open document to discuss.

2   Click **Tools**, **Online Collaboration**...... `Alt`+`T`, `N`

3   Click **Web Discussions**... `W`

> 📖   *Web Discussions may be listed more than once.*

4   Enter discussion server information, if necessary, in
     Add or Edit Discussion Server dialog box.

5   Click `Discussions ▼` .... `Alt`+`N`
     on **Discussions** toolbar.

6   Click **Insert about the Document**.......................... `N`

7   Click **Discussion subject** text box and enter
     discussion subject line.

8   Click **Discussion text** text box and type remark
     as desired.

9   Click `OK` .... `Enter`

SAVE DOCUMENT AS WEB PAGE

1   Open document to save as Web page.

2   Click **File**, **Save as Web Page** .... `Alt`+`F`,`G`

3   Type **File name**, if necessary .... *filename*

To change Web page's title:

   a   Click `Change Title...` .... `Alt`+`C`

   b   Type **Page title**, as desired .... *title*

   c   Click `OK` .... `Enter`

4   Click `Save` .... `Enter`

A

align
objects 136
   relative to page 137
page (vertical) 103
text (shortcuts) 105
   text wrapping 143
   using menu 107, 124
   using ruler 106, 124
apply style......................110
shortcuts 112
arrange all windows................2
attach template 14
AutoCorrect 191
AutoFit 158
AutoFormat......................120
apply 120
as you type 123
options 122
review changes............121
table 170
AutoShapes......................127
add text to 144
draw 127
AutoSum..........................168
AutoText 51
delete entry 52
insert entry 51-52
Organizer 117

B

background......................53
colors 57-58
gradient......................54
pattern........................56
picture........................57
texture........................55
theme..........................53
begin online meeting 231
bookmark..........................171
delete 171
go to 172
border..........................59-62
graphic object
   color 140

style..........................141
weight..........................141
text box......................144
bound document 100, 89
break, insert 96-97
shortcuts 96
browse folders (Word) 16
find files 18
navigate (shortcuts) 17
bulleted list......................64
customize....................66
multilevel list..............70
   customize................71
bullets..............................80

C

caption 172
case (letter case) 74
cell (table)
delete 156
insert 154
insert tabs in..............164
merge..........................163
reference....................167
split............................163
chain (link text boxes) 145
character
formatting....................73
position........................78
spacing........................77
check box............................5
citation, mark 188
clear tab stop 125
clip art 129-132
download....................131
gallery 129-132
import into gallery..........131
insert 129
search for 130
Clipboard toolbar 36
clear 36
paste all items from..........36
close
all files 19
document 19
color 62-63

    custom palette.................. 58
    font 76
    highlighter pen 199
    object border 140
    standard palette 57
column
    break, insert 96-7
    custom........................... 94
    delete (table) 156
    gridlines...................... 159
    insert (table) 155
    marker 98, 159
    newspaper style 93-94
        custom...................... 94
        force new.................. 95
    sizing arrow 159
    width
        adjust................. 159-160
        AutoFit..................... 158
        distribute evenly 158
command buttons 5
comments 192
    display........................ 193
    edit 193
    insert 192
    review......................... 194
compare versions............... 210
context-sensitive help 12
convert
    footnotes/endnotes 177
    text/table................ 152-153
copy and paste.................... 35
create
    AutoText entry................. 51
    custom columns 94
    custom toolbar................. 45
    style.......................... 112
    table 150
    template 14
crop object 135
crosshair pointer 128
    enhanced 139
cross-references 174
cut and paste 34

D
data source 214, 219-223
date 83, 87
day............................... 83
default setting, change
    font........................... 77
    margins........................ 99
    paper source 102
    table setup................... 151
    tab stops..................... 125
delete
    AutoText entry 52
    cells 156
    columns 156
    custom toolbar................. 46
    graphic object............... 134
    rows 156
    style 116
    tab stop......................125-6
    text........................... 37
dialog box elements 5
direction, text.................. 145
discussions...................... 232
display
    document properties 23
    full menu...................... 47
    gridlines (table)............. 150
    hidden toolbar buttons..... 42
    toolbar 42
distribute
    columns/rows 158
    objects 136
document 13
    bound 100
    close 19
    close all 19
    navigation....................25-26
    open 15
        browse...................16-18
    print.......................... 22
    properties 23
    protect 202
    save........................... 19
        as Web page 233
        browse...................16-18
        copy of (Save As) 20

version 20
select entire 28
select text.............28-29
unprotect.....................203
download clip art.................131
drag and drop 34, 35
pointer.....................34, 35
draw
AutoShape......................127
freeform object.................128
table 151
drop cap.........................75
drop-down list box 5

E
editing options 82
AutoFormat......................122
effects
fill 142
font.....................74, 76
shadow 139
3-D 139
endnote
convert 177
insert 175-176
view......................177
envelope......................212
European letters.................80
exit Microsoft Word.................1

F
field.........................83
merge.................223-224
file and folder list.................16
fill effects.........................54
colors 57-58
gradient 54
object 142
pattern......................56
picture......................57
texture......................55
find.........................195
text again 196
first-line indent marker 106
flip object 137
floating table 157
flow, text......................109

font.........................76
shortcuts......................73
size (shortcuts).................73
style (shortcuts).................74
footer.........................86
advanced......................87
edit......................88
placement 88
footnote
convert 177
insert 175-176
view......................177
force new column.................95
Format Painter.....................79
formatting
AutoFormat 120-123
character......................73
indents and spacing.......105
page.........................96
paragraph......................105
section......................96
table (AutoFormat).......170
formula (table)............167, 168
AutoSum......................168
freeform object......................127
draw......................128
edit......................139
Full Screen view 40

G
gallery *(See clip art gallery.)*
Go To 25, 172
grammar check.................203
options 205
graphic objects.............127-143
modify 134-143
gridlines.................150, 159
group objects 136

H
handles
adjustment 148
object 31, 32
rotate 137, 138
table move 157
table resize......................157
hanging-indent marker.........106

header 86
   advanced 87
   edit 88
   placement 88
headings, repeat (table) 164
Help 7
   dialog box 12
   Help menu 12
   Office Assistant 7
   window 10
hide
   gridlines (table) 150
   toolbar 42
highlighter pen 199
hyphenation 200

I
import
   file into clip gallery 131
   picture 133
increment box 5, 6
indent marker 106
indents 106-107
   buttons/shortcuts 105
index 178
   compile 181
   mark entry 178
   tab (Help feature) 10
indicator, Overtype 37
insert
   break 96
   cell (table) 154
   clip art 129
   column (table) 155
   date 83
   endnote 175
   field 83-4
   footnote 175
   formula (table) 168
   page number 89
   row (table) 154
   symbol 80
   time 83

K
kerning 77
keyboard shortcuts *(See shortcuts.)*

L
label
   caption 173
   mailing 213
landscape orientation 101
layer objects 138
layout, page 103
leading 108
left-indent marker 106
letter case 74
line
   break, insert 96-97
   numbers 103
   spacing 108
link
   text boxes 145
      move between 146
list box 5, 6

M
macro 90
   keyboard shortcut 91
   Organizer 117
   record (create) 90
   run (play) 92
   toolbar button 91
mailing label 213
mail merge 214
   advanced options 225
   data source 219, 223
   main document 215
   merge documents 225
   merge fields 223-224
   preview 224
   toolbar 217
mail, Office 229
main document 214, 215
margin 98-99
   boundary 98
   bound documents 100
   text box 145

INDEX

maximize window 1
meeting, online 230
  begin 231
  schedule 230
menus 47
  display all full 48
  display full 47
  personalized 47
merge
  cells 163
  mail merge 214-226
  revised documents 210
Microsoft Help window 10
minimize window 1
mode
  Overtype 37
modify objects
  align 136
  distribute 136
  flip 137
  order 138
  rotate 137
    freely 137
  size 134
  style 115
More Buttons arrow 42
move
  between text boxes 146
  graphic object 134
  pointer 30
  text 34
  toolbar 44

N

named tab 6
navigation
  document (shortcuts) 26
  folders (shortcuts) 17
  Go To 25
  table (shortcuts) 27
newspaper columns 93-94
  custom 95
  force new column 95
  margins 98
new window 2
nonprinting characters 49
NORMAT.DOT 13

Normal view 40
note I-beam 177
numbered lines 103
numbered list 64, 65
  customize 68
  multilevel list 70
    customize 71

O

object 127
  align 136
  AutoShapes 127
  border 140-141
  center, size from 135
  crop 135
  delete 134
  distribute 136
  fill effects 142
  flip 137
  freeform 127
    draw 128
    edit 139
  graphic 127-143
  group 136
  handles 31, 32
  modify 134
  move 134
  order 138
  proportions, maintain 135
  rotate 137
    freely 137
  select 30
  shade 141
  shadow 139
  size 134
  text box 144
  text wrapping 142
  3-D effect 139
  ungroup 136
Office Assistant 7
  hide 9
  settings 9
  show 9
  turn off 9
Office Clipboard toolbar 36
Office mail 229
online meeting 230

begin 231
schedule 230
open document 15
order, object 138
Organizer 117
copy items 118
delete items 119
rename item 119
outline
assign levels 107
view 40
Overtype mode 37

P

page
align (vertical) 103
break, insert 96-97
formatting 96
layout 103
numbers 83, 87, 89
orientation 100
setup 98
size 100
source 102
pane sizing arrow 3
paragraph formatting
buttons/shortcuts 105
line spacing 108
paragraph spacing 108
text flow 109
using menu 107
using ruler 106
picture
import 133
insert from file 133
restore 139
placeholder 83
text box, Auto Shape 144
placement, table 157
Places bar 16
portrait orientation 101
preview
box 6
merged file 224
pane 16
print 22
printer setup 23

Print Layout view 40
Print Preview 40
properties, document 23
proportion, object 135
protect document 202

R

radio button 6
record macro 90
records (merge) 214
redo 38-39
relative, align 137
remove toolbar button 43
repeat headings (table) 164
replace text 195, 197
options 196
resize *(See size.)*
restore
picture 139
window 1
review
changes 208-209
comments 194
right-indent marker 106
rotate object 137
freely 137
row (table)
delete 156
height, adjust 161
insert 154
marker 161
rulers 49
paragraph indents 106
run macro 92

S

save document 19
as Web page 233
copy of (Save As) 20
schedule meeting 230
screen
display options 50
menus 47-49
nonprinting characters 49
rulers 49
toolbars 42-46
viewing (shortcuts) 74

views........................40-41
ScreenTip 12, 36, 46
scroll bar.......................5, 6
search
   clips..........................130
   options......................196
section break, insert 96
section formatting 96
select 28-33
   cell 33
   column 32
   entire document............28
   entire table.................32
   graphic object(s) 30
   row 33
   table data...................32
   text......................28-29
   text box 31
   text box object................32
selection bar 33
semitransparent 141
set
   margins......................98
      text box 145
   paragraph alignment......107
   paragraph indents......106-8
   paragraph spacing.........107
   tab stops 124
      default stops 125
setup, printer....................23
shading......................62-63
   graphic object 141
      semitransparent........141
shadow effect 139
shortcut menus 4
shortcuts, keyboard
   font............................73
   font size 73
   font style 74
   indents and spacing......105
   insert breaks 96
   letter case 73
   navigate (document)........26
   navigate (folders)...........17
   navigate (table)..............27
   on-screen viewing.........74
   paragraph alignment......105

select (text) 29
styles, apply 112
web 227
show *(See display.)*
size
   object 134
   table 157
   toolbar 45
   window 2
sizing arrow........................2
sizing handles 30
sort text 164
   advanced options...........165
spacing...................106-107
   buttons/shortcuts.........105
   character 77
   line 108
   paragraph...................108
special character........... 80, 81
spell check......................203
   background 4
   options 205
split
   cells.........................163
   table 163
   window 3
style..............................110
   apply 110-112
   character 110
   create 112
   default 110
   delete 116
   modify 115-116
   Organizer 117
   paragraph...................110
   shortcuts 112
subscript.................... 76, 78
summary information 24
superscript 76, 78

T
tab 124
   clear stop 125-6
   insert in table cell 164
   set default stops............125
   type button 106, 124
table 150

AutoFormat 170
convert text to............... 152
convert to text............... 153
create 150
delete
   cell(s)..................... 156
   column(s)/row(s) 156
draw 151
floating.......................... 157
format 170
formulas 167, 168
   AutoSum 168
headings, repeat 164
insert 150-151
   cell(s)...................... 154
   column(s) 155
   formula 168
   row(s) 154
   tab in cell 164
move handle 157
navigate in 27
placement...................... 157
resize............................. 157
select
   cell 33
   column 32
   data in 32
   entire table 32
   row........................... 33
split............................... 163
text 164
   sort 164-166
wrap text....................... 157
table of authorities
compile.......................... 189
mark citation................. 188
table of contents
compile.......................... 184
mark entry 183
table of figures 186
taskbar 2
template 13, 14
attach document 14
create document 13
text
alignment (shortcuts) 105
convert table to............. 153

convert to table............. 152
copy 35
cut34
delete............................ 37
flow 109
move 34
paste 34
sort.......................... 164-166
wrap............... 96, 142, 157
text box (dialog box) 5, 6
text box (object).................. 144
   AutoShape, add to 144
   create 144
   illustration 5
   link 145
      move between 146
   rotate text in 145
   select 31
   select object 32
   set margins.................. 145
   text direction 145
themes............................... 53
thesaurus........................... 206
3-D effect........................... 139
time................................ 83, 87
toolbar 42
   add button 43
   create custom 45
   delete custom 46
   display 42, 44
   hidden buttons................ 42
   hide.............................. 42
   move............................ 44
   Office clipboard 36
   options......................... 46
   Organizer...................... 117
   personalized............. 42, 44
   remove button 43
   separate 44
   size.............................. 45
   Web 227
   WordArt 149
track changes...............207, 208
   compare versions........... 210
   merge revised files 210
   review changes 208-209
trademark symbol................. 80

Index

U

undo.....................................38
ungroup objects.................136
unprotect document............203
update
    document (Save).............19
    field code/result...............85

V

versions
    compare.........................210
    save.................................20
    work with.........................21
vertical page alignment......103
vertical ruler.......................49
view
    comments......................193
    field code/result...............85
    footnote/endnote............177
views
    Full Screen.......................40
    Normal.............................40
    Outline.............................40
    Print Layout......................40
    Print Preview....................40
    Web Layout......................40
    Zoom.............................41
Views button...................16, 17

W

watermark........................146
Web Layout view.................40
Web page, save as............233
Web toolbar......................227
What's This? help...............12
window
    arrange all.........................2
    close...............................19
    exit...................................1
    maximize...........................1
    minimize............................1
    move.................................2
    next..................................2
    resize...............................2
    restore..............................1
    split.................................3
WordArt.......................148-9
word count........................211
Word Help window...............10
wrap text.........................142
    insert break......................96
    table..............................157
    watermark.......................147

Z

Zoom................................41

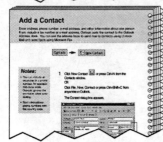

Fast-teach Learning Books

How we designed each book

Each self-paced hands-on text gives you the software concept and each exercise's objective in simple language. Next to the exercise w provide the keystrokes and the illustrated layout; step by simple step—graded and cumulative learning.

Did we make one for you?

Titles **$27 each**	Cat. No.
● Creating a Web Page with Office 97	Z23
● Corel® Office 7	Z12
● Corel® WordPerfect® 7	Z16
● Corel® WordPerfect® 8	Z31
● DOS + Windows	Z7
English Skills through Word Processing	Z34
● Excel 97	Z21
Excel 5 for Windows®	E9
Excel 7 for Windows® 95	Z11
● Internet	Z57
● Internet for Business	Z27
● Internet for Kids	Z25
● Keyboarding & Word Processing with Word 97	Z24
● Keyboarding & Word Processing for Kids	Z33
Lotus 1-2-3 Rel. 2.2–4.0 for DOS	L9
Lotus 1-2-3 Rel. 4 & 5 for Windows	B9
● Microsoft Office 97	Z19
Microsoft Office for Windows 95	Z6
● PowerPoint 97	Z22
Windows® 3.1 – A Quick Study	WQS1
Windows® 95	Z3
● Windows® 98	Z26
● Word 97	Z20
Word 6 for Windows®	1WDW6
Word 7 for Windows® 95	Z10
WordPerfect 6 for Windows®	Z9
WordPerfect 6.1 for Windows®	H9
Works 4 for Windows® 95	Z8

Microsoft® OFFICE 2000

Titles **$29 each**	Cat.
● Accounting Applications with Excel 2000	
● Access 2000	
● Create a Web Page with Office 2000	
● Computer Literacy with Office 2000	
● Excel 2000	
● FrontPage 2000	
● Keyboarding & Word Processing with Word 2000	
● Office 2000	
● Office 2000 Deluxe Edition $34	Z
*Includes advanced exercises and illust solutions for most exercises	
● Office 2000 Advanced Skills: An Integrated Approach	
● PowerPoint 2000	
● Publisher 2000	
● Windows 2000	
● Word 2000	

● Includes CD-ROM

DDC Publishing

275 Madison Ave., New York, NY

**to order call
800-528-3897
or fax 800-528-38**

Preview any of our bo
on the Web at:
www.ddcpub.com